DONALD BARRA

The
Dynamic
Performance

A Performer's Guide to Musical
Expression and Interpretation

With a Foreword by Yehudi Menuhin

Prentice-Hall, Inc., Englewood Cliffs, N.J. 07632

Library of Congress Cataloging in Publication Data

BARRA, DONALD.
   The dynamic performance.

    1. Music—Interpretation (Phrasing, dynamics,
etc.) I. Title.
MT75.B29   781.6'3   82-5366
ISBN 0-13-221556-X   AACR2

Editorial production/supervision by Peter Roberts
Cover design by Celine A. Brandes of Photo Plus Art
Manufacturing buyer: Raymond Keating

Printed in the United States of America

10 9 8 7 6 5 4 3 2 1

ISBN 0-13-221556-X

PRENTICE-HALL INTERNATIONAL, INC., *London*
PRENTICE-HALL OF AUSTRALIA PTY. LIMITED, *Sydney*
PRENTICE-HALL CANADA INC., *Toronto*
PRENTICE-HALL OF INDIA PRIVATE LIMITED, *New Delhi*
PRENTICE-HALL OF JAPAN, INC., *Tokyo*
PRENTICE-HALL OF SOUTHEAST ASIA PTE. LTD., *Singapore*
WHITEHALL BOOKS LIMITED, *Wellington, New Zealand*

Foreword

I am delighted with *The Dynamic Performance* by Donald Barra. If it did not carry Donald Barra's signature, I would be tempted to call it my own so closely do our thoughts coincide.

Donald Barra has restored music to the function of living language and saved it from the interrupted and meaningless staccato of the teletype.

He has done so on a *sound* basis—no pun intended—for his verbal arguments are irrefutable and, as all theories should be, not deforming of life but dissolving of the theory when applied into the very blood of life.

His is a bridge between intuition and reason and provides a fruitful feedback to intuition, strengthening it and keeping it within the bounds of good taste.

All my gratitude, all my congratulations, all my relief for having released me from the need of writing his book!

Yehudi Menuhin

Contents

Preface   vii

chapter 1
Basic Principles of Expression   1

Chapter 1 examines the fundamental principles of musical expression, discusses the relationship of the expressive elements, and explains how these elements can be used to reinforce the character, style, and emotional tone of a composition.

chapter 2
Phrasing   18

Chapter 2 explains the basic concept of the musical phrase, discusses the factors that determine the shape of a developing musical impulse, and illustrates different kinds of tonal development.

chapter 3
Patterns of Evolution   46

Chapter 3 discusses the effect of melodic contour, harmonic structure, motific relationships, metric structure, and style on the phrasing of compositions.

chapter 4
Rhythm and Meter   74

Chapter 4 deals with the relationship of rhythm and meter on the higher levels of musical structure and explains how the shaping of certain ''key'' phrases can determine the dynamic form of an entire musical sequence.

chapter 5
Rubato   99

Chapter 5 examines the basic concept of rubato, explains the nature of various upbeat and afterbeat patterns, and illustrates how to use rubato to reinforce the development of higher-level sequences.

chapter 6
The Dynamic Impulse   123

Chapter 6 focuses upon complete compositions. It illustrates how certain aspects of a work help to create its dramatic shape, and how the position of a particular phrase helps to determine its function in relation to the dynamic evolution of the entire piece.

chapter 7
Performance Techniques   158

Chapter 7 examines expressive techniques in relation to the major performance areas. It discusses the application of these techniques in terms of the piano, strings, winds, voice, and instrumental and choral conducting.

Index of Musical Examples   177

Preface

It is a cliché in our profession that a performer can accurately reproduce all of the notes of a composition and still produce very little music. It is generally understood that the reproduction of sounds is only the first step in any serious interpretive effort. To produce significant results the performer must bring to light those expressive qualities and dynamic characteristics that are contained *within* the musical structure. His ultimate goal must be to translate the musical symbols into vibrant, meaningful patterns of motion that will reach directly to the heart and mind of the listener and trigger his intuitive positive response.

It is generally agreed, of course, that there is no single, "correct" way to interpret a particular composition. There is no question as to the truth of that statement. Indeed, most pieces are amenable to a variety of interpretations, and their performance often varies significantly, even when played by the same performing artist. But by the same token it is also true that all interpretations are not equally valid, that some are better than others, and that all serious artists spend a good deal of time trying to improve their interpretation of the works they perform.

And yet of all the various aspects of music theory, this process of musical expression and interpretation is among the least understood. As a result, young performers in particular often lack the conceptual tools to make an intelligent interpretive analysis.

The following text was written in an effort to help overcome this deficiency. It was developed in the belief that an understanding of the principles of expression and interpretation will enable the performer to create a more vivid realization of the musical score. The examples presented here are not intended as inflexible prescriptions, but as illustrations of those solutions that are possible, given the dynamic forces that are inherent in any particular composition.

It is hoped that the performance diagrams presented in this book will provide the performer with a general method of operation—a plan of attack and a means of analysis—that will help him to realize his own musical ideas more effectively. These diagrams will not, of course, replace his own good musical judgment; yet they may help him to discover certain dynamic implications that are hidden within the fabric of tones—implications that are, in fact, the most essential feature of every significant musical structure.

ACKNOWLEDGMENTS

I would like to thank my colleagues at the University of Pittsburgh and at Indiana University of Pennsylvania for their contribution to the development of this text. I would especially like to thank Tamra Saylor for her invaluable help and encouragement through what seemed to be at times an unending succession of early drafts. Many of her suggestions and comments have been incorporated, directly and indirectly, into the final version of this book.

Donald Barra

CHAPTER 1

Basic Principles
of Expression

√The most important relationship in music, for performer and listener alike, is that which exists between *tension* and *energy*. Tension, in music, is created by the patterns that exist within the musical structure, or more correctly, by the listener's efforts to grasp those patterns and anticipate their evolution. Musical energy, on the other hand, is a more objective, measurable phenomenon. It is determined by the loudness, pace, resonance, and pitch of the sound and is contained directly within the tonal impulse.)

√**The central act of musical expression and interpretation lies in the performer's ability to adjust the energy elements of the tonal impulse in a way that enhances and reinforces the patterns of tension that are an inherent·part of every musical structure.**)

STYLE

The above principle holds true on both the general and the specific levels of musical development. Every experienced performer understands, for example, that tempo and dynamic markings do not mean the same thing in

EX. 1 Haydn, *Symphony No. 104,* 2nd mvt.

2

every musical context. An adagio of Mozart is not that of Bruckner or
Mahler. In example 1, despite the sforzando markings, the accents of the
Haydn melody must be more restrained than those of the Tchaikowsky
melody in example 2 or the Davidovsky excerpt of example 3. The contrasts of dynamics and pace in the Haydn must be more moderate, the expressive shadings more contained, the fluctuations less obvious.

EX. 2   Tchaikowsky, *Symphony No. 6 (Pathètique)*, 1st mvt.

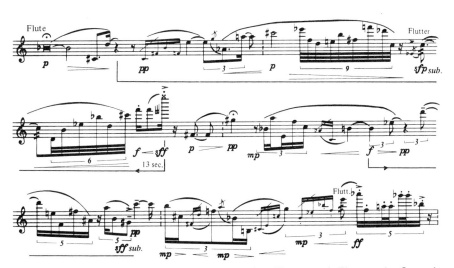

EX. 3   Davidovsky, *Synchronisms No. 1 for Flute and Electronic Sounds*
(Copyright 1965, 1967 by Josef Marx; used by permission of McGinnis
and Marx Publishers.)

Articulation, too, must be geared to the musical context. The staccato of the Wagner melody in example 4 must be shorter, tighter, and more forceful than that of the Haydn melody of example 1.

The legato of the theme from *Romeo and Juliet* in example 5 must be more expansive than that of the Bach Andante in example 6.

More complex, irregular, high-tension structures require more dramatic contrasts of energy, color, and articulation, whereas other more balanced, lower-tension structures naturally call for a more restrained approach.

Homeostasis

The principle of expression described above is based upon a process of physiological equilibrium called *homeostasis,* which concerns the way in which the body responds to external stimuli. Like other animal species, human beings have a basic physiological activity rate at which their neurological and metabolic functions normally occur. Stimuli that match this rate tend to create ''moderate'' sensory impressions. Those that do not match this rate seem loud or soft, fast or slow, warm or cold, according to their sphere of sensory influence.

Psychologists have discovered that people tend to prefer stimuli that match (and thus reinforce) their levels of physiological activity. For example, subjects at normal levels of alertness usually characterize the median stimuli as the most pleasant, those at the low end of the scale as less pleasant, and those at the high-energy extreme as least pleasant.[1] However people also tend to seek out and enjoy high-energy stimulation when they are in a more excited state, and they tend to prefer low-energy stimulation when they are in a more relaxed frame of mind. These changes directly reflect, and reinforce, our moods and feelings.[2]

These relationships help to establish the basic mood or emotional tone of a composition. Pieces that contain moderate amounts of energy, for example, may seem to lack any specific mood. As energy levels move toward the extremes, impressions become more pronounced. Compositions that contain high amounts of energy may seem exciting, exuberant, or even frenzied. Those that contain low amounts of energy may seem calm, relaxed, or lethargic. In this way compositions can reflect the entire range of emotional intensity.

---

[1] This principle extends to the harmonic realm. That is to say, people normally identify the median-energy tertian intervals as more pleasant than either the low-energy perfect intervals or the high-energy dissonant intervals.

[2] They also affect our perceptions. In the excitement of performance, for example, a performer may choose a faster tempo than he would normally assign to a particular piece, a miscalculation that can have unfortunate consequences!

EX. 4 Wagner, *Die Meistersinger,* Overture

EX. 5 Tchaikowsky, *Romeo and Juliet,* Overture-Fantasy

EX. 6 Bach, *Brandenburg Concerto No. 4,* 2nd mvt.

However, as we mentioned earlier, every composition also contains *its own* patterns of tension as determined by the complexity, range, and depth of its tonal relationships. Here it is the relationship to median energy levels that is the principal determining factor. As a rule, more complex, high-tension structures require greater contrasts of energy, phrasing, and articulation than low-tension structures, for it is the precise point of balance *between* tension and energy that produces the optimum aesthetic effect.[3]

DIVERGENT ENERGY PATTERNS

The situation is complicated by the fact that musical energy is not a simple, monolithic entity. Tonal energy is made up of four different attributes: loudness, pace, timbre, and pitch, and the levels of these attributes may or may not coincide within a particular composition.)

The introduction to Rimsky-Korsakov's tone poem *Scheherazade*, for instance, contains two themes, each based upon a different energy profile. In the first theme (example 7), which represents a powerful, authoritative sultan, the tonal attributes are at opposite ends of the energy spectrum. The music is loud (high energy ↑) but slow (low energy ↓), rich in timbre (high energy ↑) but low in pitch (low energy ↓).

EX. 7 Rimsky-Korsakov, *Scheherazade*, "Sultan's theme"

In the second theme (example 8), which represents the sultan's young bride, Scheherazade, the tonal attributes also diverge, but in the opposite direction. Here the music is soft (low energy ↓) but quite fast (high energy ↑), "thin" in timbre (low energy ↓) but high in pitch (high energy ↑).[4]

These contrasting energy patterns are crucial to the expressive character of the music.) The first theme, for instance, seems massive, weighty, and voluminous. It projects a musical image that is entirely fitting

[3] For a more detailed discussion of homeostasis, see Hans and Shulamith Kreitler's *Psychology of the Arts* (Durham, N.C.: Duke University Press, 1972), pp. 12–26, and Terrance McLaughlin's *Music and Communication* (New York: St. Martin's Press, 1970).

[4] Although it is not usually thought of in such terms, timbre, too, is energy. The amount of timbre-energy depends largely upon the complexity of the acoustical signal, and varies from the low-energy, "thin" sound of flutes and tuning forks to the high-energy brass, cymbals, and noise. Pitch-energy varies from slow to fast vibration rates.

EX. 8 Rimsky-Korsakov, *Scheherazade,* "Scheherazade's theme"

for an authoritative sultan. The second theme seems gentle, small, and graceful—an image that is much more appropriate for Scheherazade.

In each of these progressions it is the particular *pattern of energy* that creates the basic expressive effect) In the next theme (example 9), from Dvořák's *New World Symphony,* the music is also loud (high energy ↑) but

EX. 9 Dvořák, *New World Symphony,* 4th mvt.

quite slow (low energy ↓), rich in timbre (high energy ↑) but rather low in pitch (low energy ↓). Once again the music seems powerful, weighty, and authoritative.

At the beginning of Mendelssohn's *Midsummer Night's Dream* (example 10), the tonal motion is soft (low energy ↓) but fast (high energy ↑), thin in timbre (low energy ↓) but high in pitch (high energy ↑). Here again the music seems light and tiny, almost weightless.

EX. 10   Mendelssohn, Overture to *Midsummer Night's Dream*

These same characterizations are evident in speech as well as in music. For example, we can speak in a big, gruff voice, one that is loud (↑) but slow (↓), rich (↑) and low-pitched (↓); or we can speak in a tiny voice, one which is soft (↓) but fast (↑), thin (↓) and high-pitched (↑).

Like the sultan's theme, the first vocal characterization seems massive, weighty, and authoritative. Its use by rough, "heavy" characters has made it a dramatic stereotype, such as Papa Bear in the children's story, "The Three Bears." The second vocal characterization seems tiny, weak, and timid—much more appropriate for Baby Bear!

Many compositions contain these energy profiles, and they exhibit these same expressive traits. The most important point here is that the performer can alter the character of the music by adjusting the ratio of these primary tonal attributes. For example, the sense of tonal weight in the "New World" melody and the sultan's theme can be enhanced by *decreasing* the tempo and/or *increasing* the volume of the music, but only up to a point, for this eventually results in a loss of thrust that detracts from the developing momentum.

Similarly, the sense of lightness and grace in the Mendelssohn and Scheherazade themes may be enhanced by *increasing* the tempo and/or *decreasing* the volume. (Once again, however, there comes a point of declining effectiveness, when the music becomes so fast and/or soft that it loses its sense of clarity and articulation.)

The goal in each case is to find that particular *balance* of weight and momentum that will most effectively enhance the *unique* character of *each* musical structure. The performer must try to find that specific point of equilibrium that will realize the composition's peak musical potential. He must try to discover what seems to be the point of maximum effect according to the patterns of motion that are an inherent part of that particular piece.

The Musical "Laws of Motion"

The dynamic principles we've been describing are based upon a physical law that was first set forth in Newton's *Second Law of Motion.* According to this law, the mass of a moving object equals its momentum divided by its velocity. In other words, large, heavy objects tend to move with relatively greater force and less speed, while smaller, lighter objects tend to move with relatively less force and greater speed; and as the mass of an object increases, this difference increases in direct proportion.

The same is true of tonal motion. That is to say, loud, slow-moving tonal impulses *sound* weighty and voluminous, whereas soft, fast-moving tonal actions sound light, tiny, and less massive. And here too, the weight of a tonal action can be increased or decreased by a proportional increase or decrease in the ratio of these attributes.[5]

The problem for the performer is to establish that combination of attributes that will most effectively reinforce the *musical* character of a particular progression. The sixth movement from Mussorgsky's *Pictures at an Exhibition* provides a good illustration of this problem (example 11A). Like *Scheherazade,* this movement is based upon two contrasting themes, each representing a different dramatic personality, in this case a rich man and a beggar. Here the tempo and dynamic levels of the music are marked in general terms, *andante* and *forte,* respectively.

---

[5] These associations are so well established that a mismatch can be very amusing. It is humorous, for example, when a large, heavy man speaks in a "tiny" voice, or when a child speaks in a "big" gruff voice, since these aural profiles do not at all reflect their physical and psychological characteristics. In a similar way, the tonal profiles of the sultan and Scheherazade directly reflect their physical and psychological attributes, and a mismatch of these associations would also be out of place.

EX. 11A Mussorgsky, "Samuel Goldenberg and Schmuyle," from *Pictures at an Exhibition*

The question is, just how fast and how loud should the music be performed? The performer might try different combinations, perhaps ♩=63 along with a moderately strong dynamic level. This produces a strong, compact impression. Or he might try ♩=50 along with a somewhat louder dynamic level. In the latter case the weight of the music is increased but the momentum is somewhat lessened.[6]

Other factors affect these considerations. One of the most important is the nature of the second theme of the movement (example 11B). This melody, which represents the beggar in the transaction, has a repetitive, nagging character that is enhanced, in the orchestrated version, by the brash, penetrating quality of muted trumpets. If the tempo of the music is taken too slowly, this melody loses its needling quality.

Of course it is possible to take a different tempo for each theme. Such tempo changes are particularly effective in larger works, for then the

---

[6] Incidentally, the momentum in the beginning of this theme can be enhanced by delaying the 64th notes slightly, and by placing them closer to their notes of release; and in the second part of the theme by increasing the pace in the anacrusis of each phrase. These and other rubato techniques are discussed in Chapter 5.

EX. 11B

unique character of each theme can be emphasized through a different energy profile. Here, however, any gross change of tempo would distort one theme or the other, for both melodies appear simultaneously later in the movement (example 11C).

EX. 11C

Secondary Elemental Combinations

In the musical excerpts we have just analyzed, the attributes of resonance and pitch tend to reinforce those of loudness and pace. This kind of correlation tends to produce strong, clear-cut dramatic images. However, other energy patterns produce other expressive effects. In the theme from the *Pathètique Symphony* (example 12), the music is loud (↑) but slow (↓), "thin" in resonance (↓) but high in pitch (↑). The expansive quality of this theme results largely from the combination of high pitch and slow pace. These energy profiles often have a soaring, floating quality about them which is reinforced by their long, smooth, flowing lines of motion. Here the proportion of weight and momentum is critical to the expressive character of the music *and* the dynamic evolution of the theme.

EX. 12   Tchaikowsky, *Symphony No. 6 (Pathètique),* 1st mvt.

A very different balance is called for in the third movement of Berg's *Lyric Suite* (example 13). Here the music is soft (↓) but fast (↑), rich in timbre (played *am steg* or "at the bridge"—↑) but moderately low in pitch (↓). Because of its rich tone quality, irregular rhythms, dissonant texture, and the absence of any clearly defined motive patterns, the music seems full of suppressed excitement, tension, and mystery. It is as if the real force behind its high levels of tension is simply waiting for the right opportunity to burst out upon us. Care must be taken here to maintain the intensity of the music despite the soft dynamics, so as to prepare for the strong release of energy that occurs at the climax of the movement.

Allegro misterioso ♩ =150

EX. 13 Berg, *Lyric Suite*, 3rd mvt. (*Copyright 1927 by Universal Edition. Copyright renewed 1955 by Helen Berg. Used by permission of European American Music Distributors Corporation, sole U.S. agent for Universal Edition.*)

A similar situation occurs at the beginning of the Bartok progression in example 14. Here the suppressed energy and excitement are eventually released in a sequence of fortissimo phrases beginning in measure 44. At this point, as in most climaxes, the music moves into a series of clear, symmetrical patterns, reinforcing the thrust of the musical impulse and resolving the listeners' perceptual efforts and pent-up tensions. Special care must be taken in these contexts to avoid the premature arrival of full intensity, for here loudness serves both to reinforce the developing momentum and, ultimately, to trigger the release of the pent-up tension and thrust.

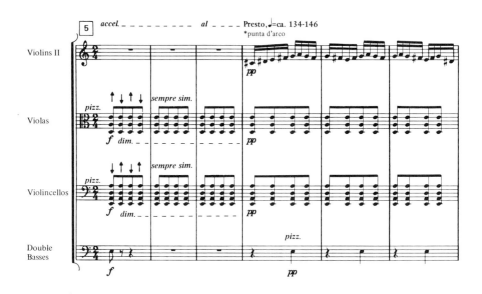

EX. 14 Bartok, *Concerto for Orchestra*, 5th mvt. *(Copyright 1946 by Hawkes & Son (London) Ltd., renewed 1973. Reprinted by permission of Boosey & Hawkes, Inc.)*

EX. 14 (continued)

The energy profiles of the preceding compositions are graphically illustrated in Figure 1.

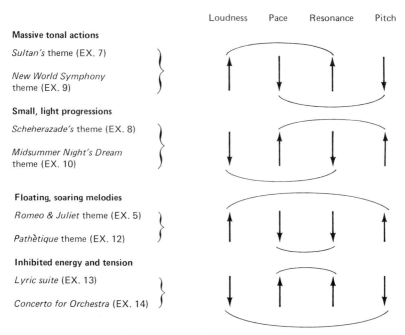

FIGURE 1.   Divergent Energy Profiles. (Other energy profiles are possible, of course, but the basic principle remains the same. In each case the performer must balance the weight of the musical action against its sense of forward thrust so as to produce that blend of tension and energy that will most effectively reinforce its inherent musical potential.)

THE SALIENT STRUCTURAL CHARACTERISTICS

1 Harmonic structure
2 Shape of rhy pattern
3 Quality of melodic growth
4 Dynam. charac. of tonal relationships

The dynamic proportions that are appropriate for a particular progression ultimately depend, of course, upon the salient features of that particular musical structure. The expressive potential of any piece depends upon the nature of its harmonic structure, the shape of its rhythmic patterns, the quality of its melodic growth, and the dynamic character of its tonal relationships.

The power and authority of the "New World" and "sultan" themes, for example, are implied by their narrow range, their repetitive tonal patterns, and their insistent emphasis on the strong beats of the measure. The grace and beauty of Scheherazade's theme are implied by its free-flowing triplets, changing rhythmic patterns, and wide-ranging arpeggio figures. The expansive lyricism of the "Pathètique" theme depends largely upon the continuity and sweep of its melodic line and the dynamic implications of its harmonic patterns. The needling character of the beggar's theme arises from its annoyingly repetitive tonal and rhythmic impulses and from its limited melodic range.

The expressive implications of each of these themes can be enhanced by emphasizing these salient structural characteristics. That is to say, the power and authority of the "New World" and "sultan" themes can be reinforced by maintaining the regularity of the meter, accenting each tone of the melody, and by centering each impulse squarely on the downbeat of the measure. This helps to create a sense of consistency, inevitability, and determination. The Scheherazade melody, on the other hand, should be played with more subtle dynamic inflections, in a flexible tempo, so as to enhance its freedom of motion and evolution. The "Pathètique" theme should maintain a continuous flow of sound, with no gaps or breaks between the individual tones of the melody. The natural thrust of the Mendelssohn and Bartok themes can be reinforced by a constant forward motion, a continuous "pressing on" of the tonal impulse. The same is true of the individual motivic thrusts of the beggar's theme. Here the rhythmic impetus should be focused on the central point of each motivic impulse to underscore its repetitive, nagging character. In each case the performer must discover and accentuate those *particular* characteristics that underlie the *unique* dynamic qualities of each musical progression.

One of the most important parts of this process, we have seen, is the ability to *independently* vary the primary tonal attributes. Unfortunately this capacity isn't always exploited. The playing of novice musicians, for instance, is often characterized by convergent energy patterns. In their performances, a change in one attribute is matched by similar changes in the others, and "loud" is thought also to mean "fast," and "soft" to mean "slow." In the same way, a rise in pitch is automatically accompanied by a crescendo and a descent by a diminuendo. As a result, their performances often sound monotonous, mechanical, and unexpressive.[7]

In a dynamic performance, these tonal attributes are continually geared to the character of the musical action and the momentum of the musical impulse. They are shaped so as to enhance the expressive tone of the musical structure and reinforce the dynamic thrust that is an inherent part of the progression. The ability to independently vary the primary tonal attributes is thus one of the most essential skills of musical expression and interpretation.

[7] This is not surprising, since the sounds of most mechanical objects tend to conform to this kind of flat, one-dimensional energy plane. As the energy input of a siren is increased, for example, the sound becomes louder, faster, higher, and more shrill. As the energy decreases, all of the tonal attributes decrease simultaneously.

There is one major exception to this general rule, however, and that is the sound of the human voice. Human beings have developed the ability to *independently* vary the basic tonal attributes and so can create a wide variety of expressive vocal images.

Present-day instruments are designed to incorporate this flexibility. Although earlier musical instruments are generally limited in flexibility as well as in range, more recent instruments have a far greater capacity to independently vary the basic tonal attributes and so possess a far greater range of expressive capabilities.

CHAPTER 2

Phrasing

The most important relationship in music is tension and energy.

In the area of interpretation, the most important quality of any musical action is its sense of forward momentum or thrust.

The most important relationship in music, we have said, is that which exists between *tension* and *energy*.) The relationship between these two elements is the primary factor in establishing the style and character of a performance, and in determining the quality and depth of the listener's response.)

This same relationship plays a fundamental role in the phrasing of compositions. In this area of interpretation, the most important quality of any musical action is its sense of forward momentum or thrust.) Controlling this momentum—nurturing, reinforcing, guiding, shaping, and ultimately resolving it—is one of the most crucial aspects of any musical performance.

DEVELOPING THE MUSICAL LINE

The key element in the phrasing of a musical composition is the performer's ability to create a sense of purposeful motion toward and away from specific points of reference on every level of musical development.) As momentum is generated from within the musical action, the tonal thrust must be carefully developed through a series of overlapping impulses, each containing its own pattern of growth, culmination, and release.

The musical phrase itself, for example, is based upon the principle of the dynamic curve. Typically, tonal actions begin with an anacrusis, or growth phase of increasing energy, reach a focal point of highest intensity, then end with a concluding phase, a release or relaxation. The focal point may occur near the beginning or the end of the phrase, to produce beginning-accented or end-accented tonal impulses. These internal phrases normally form several higher-level cycles of motion, each with its own pattern of development.)

The Bach excerpt in example 15A, for instance, is based upon a series of three internal impulses that combine to form a single end-accented phrase, as indicated by the arrows above the staff. This pattern is repeated throughout the first section of the piece.

EX. 15A   Bach, *Suite in F Major,* Bourrée

When these phrase patterns are articulated in performance, they prepare the way for an expansion of the sequence that occurs in the middle section of the piece. Reinforcement of these patterns helps to unite the two sections into a single musical impulse (example 15B).

EX. 15B

In the next Haydn excerpt (example 16A), two short, beginning-accented impulses are followed by a single end-accented thrust to form a series of higher-level phrases.

The clear articulation of this dynamic pattern prepares the way for a stronger reinforcement of these impulses later in the movement, again helping to underscore the evolution of the higher-level sequences (example 16B).

EX. 16A Haydn, *Symphony No. 104,* 4th mvt.

EX. 16B

Example 17 is based upon a series of internal impulses that form a single higher-level melodic curve. Here the thrust of the music ultimately reaches to the high point of the sequence on the downbeat of measure 5, then falls gradually through a series of descending intervals to the downbeat of measure 8.

EX. 17 Beethoven, *Piano Sonata in C Minor (Pathètique),* Op. 13, 3rd mvt.

Alternative Patterns of Interpretation

The dynamic form of a phrase is created by a number of different factors. The contour of the melodic line, the rhythmic patterns, the harmonic structure, the metric relationships, non-harmonic tones, wide intervalic leaps, altered tones—all these serve to establish the fundamental curve that is an inherent part of every tonal pattern. In fact *anything* in the musical structure that tends to draw attention toward one tone and away from another helps to determine the dynamic form of the musical impulse. But these factors don't always coincide, and as a result the same phrase may sometimes be interpreted in several different ways.

In the case of conflicting interpretive possibilities, the performer should as a rule choose those alternatives that serve to reinforce the higher-level patterns of development. One way this can be accomplished, surprisingly enough, is by *suppressing* the resolution of certain initial impulses, and by then expanding, reinforcing, and ultimately resolving them later on in the progression.

This principle of interpretation is illustrated in example 18A, taken from Tchaikowsky's Fourth Symphony. The primary focal point of the motive in this example might be centered on the first or the second downbeat of the phrase. The first interpretation is supported by the downward curve of the melody and the nonharmonic tone on the first downbeat of the phrase. The second interpretation is supported by the leap of a perfect fourth (or fifth) at the end of the impulse.

Either this . . .

or this . . .

EX. 18A   Tchaikowsky, *Symphony No. 4,* 2nd mvt.

22

Which interpretation is best? The answer lies in the development of the second half of the theme. Here the principal motive reappears in a partially inverted form that clearly reinforces the *second* pattern of development (example 18B).

EX. 18ʙ

In this case it is better to shape the initial motive with the focal point on the *first* downbeat of the phrase, for this creates a suppressed dynamic tendency (indicated by the dotted arrow in example 18C) that can be reinforced later in the sequence. Suppressing the release of this impulse at the beginning of the progression creates a reservoir of tension, along with a strong expectation of its eventual resolution, that helps to fuel the development of the entire musical sequence.

EX. 18ᴄ

This interpretive strategy is also effective in example 19A, from Beethoven's Eighth Symphony. Here the second motive of the sequence might be shaped with the principal accent on the first high point of the impulse (the downbeat of measure 3) or on the second high point (the downbeat of measure 4). The first interpretation is supported by the appoggiatura figure in the melody. The second is supported by the rising melodic line and the descending pattern in the bass.

Either this . . .

or this . . .

EX. 19A   Beethoven, *Symphony No. 8,* 1st mvt.

Which interpretation is best? Once again the solution depends upon the rest of the progression. In this case the rising scale pattern serves as the basis for the development of the entire sequence. This rising impulse first occurs in measure 1, then in measures 3, 5, and 9, and finally in the bass in measure 10, as shown in example 19B.

EX. 19B

EX. 19B (continued)

Here it is better to shape the motive with the principal accent on the downbeat of measure 3, for this creates a suppressed dynamic tendency that can be reinforced gently in measure 5, and then more strongly at the end of the sequence, where it becomes the primary impetus for the final musical thrust (example 19C).

EX. 19C

The same strategy can be used in the Stravinsky theme in example 20A. Here the focal point of the phrase might be placed on the first tone of the motive, which falls on the downbeat of measure 1, or on the highest tone, which occurs at a weaker metric position.

Either this . . .

or this . . .

EX. 20A   Stravinsky, *Symphony of Psalms,* 2nd mvt. *(Copyright 1931 by Edition Russe de Musique, renewed 1958. Copyright and renewal assigned to Boosey & Hawkes, Inc. Revised edition copyright 1948 Boosey & Hawkes, Inc. Renewed 1975. Reprinted by Boosey & Hawkes, Inc.)*

Here again, suppression of the rising impulse (in measure 1 and again in measure 3) creates an inhibited dynamic tendency that can be reinforced in the following phrases (example 20B). (In this case special care must be taken to measure the precise perceptual weight of each tone, for higher tones tend to stand out stronger than lower tones, and their level of emphasis must be adjusted in relation to the dynamic form of the entire sequence.)

EX. 20B

In Bach's *Invention No. 1* the emphasis might be placed on the first or the last high point of the motive (example 21A).

Either this . . .

EX. 21A   Bach, *Invention No. 1 in C Major*

or this . . .

EX. 21A (continued)

Here again the first interpretation is best, for it contains a suppressed dynamic thrust that can be exploited later in the piece. The thrust of this impulse is reinforced in various cadential sequences (example 21B) and later by an extension of its final tone (example 21C).

EX. 21B

EX. 21C

The thrust of this embryonic impulse is finally resolved at the end of the piece (example 21D). Here the momentum of the music should be extended to the high point of the piece, the tonic C in measure 20, and then into and through the final cadential release, so as to completely fulfill all of the earlier suppressed dynamic tendencies and implications.

EX. 21ᴅ

THE PSYCHOLOGICAL THEORY OF EMOTIONS

The principle of interpretation we have been discussing is based upon a theory of emotions developed near the turn of the century by several eminent psychologists. According to this theory, feeling arises from our inhibited or suppressed desires and expectations. The theory is based upon the fact that a certain amount of nervous energy or excitation is produced by our expectations. When these expectations are unfulfilled, the nervous energy is denied an outlet and is retained in the form of tension. This inhibited energy, or tension, forms the basis of our emotional response.

As we have seen, every musical structure contains its own particular pattern of tensive development. Listeners who are sensitive to these patterns become actively involved in the musical process. As these listeners respond to the tonal impulse they automatically begin to anticipate the development of its tonal forms, project its course, and look forward to its resolution. As tension builds, these listeners experience the intensity and quality of the musical action as an integral part of their own perceptual response.[1]

---

[1] It is important, from a theoretical point of view, to distinguish between our cognitive expectations, which are normally centered in the left hemisphere of the brain, and our more reflexive perceptual anticipations and projections, which are centered in the right hemisphere. For example, we can be surprised by the ending of a play or novel only once, but the completion of a musical composition can still feel fresh and new after any number of hearings. The fact that our perceptual responses are largely reflexive enables us to respond to the same progression any number of times. It means that familiar syncopations still feel imbalanced, that unfinished melodic patterns still sound incomplete, and that irregular harmonic resolutions still seem ''deceptive,'' even though we have heard them many times before. The performer can reinforce this sense of freshness by drawing attention to these imbalances, and by continually shedding new light on their relationship to the overall musical structure.

According to the Psychological Theory of Emotions, tensions and expectations must be sustained *for a sufficient period of time* if they are to become the basis of significant emotional reactions. It is not simply the development of tension, but the *prolongation* of tension, that is the basis of our deeply felt emotional experiences.

In music, tension can be sustained only through the gradual expansion and development of an ongoing musical line. The performer must extend the musical thrust beyond the interior phrases of the composition. He must not only shape each phrase according to its inherent dynamic patterns, he must also adjust these patterns in a way that reinforces the development of the higher-level musical actions. He must focus his care and attention on every internal impulse, but he must always keep in mind the dynamic evolution of the entire composition.[2]

Strategies of Interpretation

This entire process can be enhanced through the initial suppression and eventual reinforcement of certain fundamental dynamic tendencies that are contained within the early phases of a progression. Compositions are often based upon incomplete, irregular, or imbalanced musical patterns that are developed and expanded during the course of the work. The performer must exploit these irregularities so as to reinforce the ongoing evolution of the piece.

The dramatic impact of the climax in the early measures of Wagner's Prelude to *Tristan und Isolde* (example 22A), for example, depends largely upon a suppressed dynamic tendency that is produced by the rising chromatic line and unstable harmony at the end of the first impulse. This unresolved motion creates a powerful, inhibited thrust that is focused on the third downbeat of the phrase.

EX. 22A   Wagner, Prelude to *Tristan und Isolde*

[2] For a more detailed discussion of the Psychological Theory of Emotions, see Leonard Meyer, *Emotion and Meaning in Music* (Chicago: The University of Chicago Press, 1956), pp. 13–42.

The motive is repeated in a rising sequence and expanded to a four-measure phrase, but its final thrust is not resolved; it is only aggravated by the extension of the initial anacrusis, the addition of a sforzando accent, and the dramatic, pregnant silences that are interspersed between each motivic statement (example 22B).

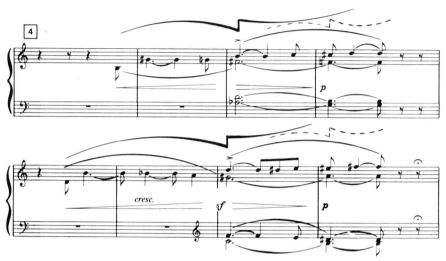

EX. 22ʙ

The last half of this motive is then exploited more fully, and its thrust is finally reinforced in the last measures of the sequence. Here the harmony is resolved, not to an A major, but to a deceptive F major chord that supports a sharply dissonant appoggiatura figure in the melody. The dramatic effect is one of soulful, romantic yearning, suppressed desires, and bittersweet resolutions (example 22C).[3]

EX. 22ᴄ

[3] Composers as well as performers should understand this concept, for much of the empty rhetoric that pervades second-rate compositions stems from the fact that these works possess no significant inhibited tendencies, which means that there is really nothing left to work out in the main body of the piece. As a result, the development of ideas often seems purely intellectual. These pieces fail to involve the listener on a deep emotional level.

Suppressed dynamic tendencies such as these are often "programed" into the score by the composer. In the Adagietto of Mahler's Fifth Symphony, for example, a number of suppressed resolutions are created by sudden shifts in the dynamic level of the music (example 23A—here a (U) above the score indicates the appearance of a sudden, unaccented release).

EX. 23A   Mahler, *Symphony No. 5*, Adagietto

These suppressed releases prepare the way for a powerful climax later in the movement (example 23B).

EX. 23B

Syncopations produce similar effects. In example 24A a series of weak-beat syncopations draws attention away from the anticipated down-beats, producing another series of suppressed resolutions. This pattern is then expanded to a four-measure phrase whose thrust is focused upon the dotted half note trill.

EX. 24A   Haydn, *Symphony No. 104,* 3rd mvt.

Later in the movement the syncopations are reinforced by the exag-gerated octave position of the tones (measures 42 and 44). The increased thrust of this impulse is at first completely suppressed (on the first beats of measures 45 and 46) and then, at the end of the last forte sequence, re-solved (example 24B).

EX. 24B

EX. 24B (continued)

Syncopations enhance the intensity of a sequence, but they don't alter its fundamental shape. In example 25, a series of offbeat accents in measures 2, 4, 6, and 8 serve to reinforce the thrust of the suppressed, secondary dynamic tendencies in these bars. The syncopations in bars 11 and 12 strongly enhance the momentum of the last sequence.

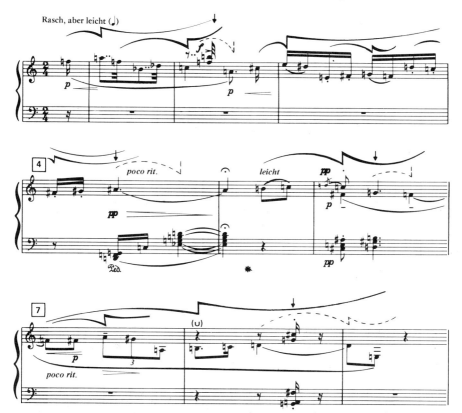

EX. 25 Schoenberg, *Sechs Kleine Klavierstücke*, Op. 19 No. 4. (*Copyright Belmont Music Publishers. Used by permission.*)

EX. 25 (continued)

In example 26, tension is created by a related technique, the sudden *overemphasis* of a projected downbeat release. In this example a strong, inhibited dynamic tendency is created by the harmonic thrust of the chordal sequence in measures 5–6, 7–8, 9–10, and 12–13. This inhibited thrust is not reinforced; instead it is aggravated by the sudden forte-piano that occurs on the downbeat of measure 13. In this case the momentum of the initial phrases should be held in check (as indicated by the parentheses

EX. 26 Beethoven, *Symphony No. 4,* 1st mvt.

around the arrows) in preparation for the sudden over-accentuation. The sequence should be played at peak intensity but with minimum force so as to create an air of mystery and suspense, which is momentarily interrupted by the arrival of the unanticipated dynamic impact.

Vocal Patterns of Expression

Phrasing is particularly problematic in vocal music, for the natural accents of the text add yet another element to the set of dynamic influences. Normally these linguistic accents simply coincide with those of the melody. In these circumstances, performance problems are concerned with the application of common vocal techniques.

In the ''Hallelujah Chorus'' (example 27), for instance, the emphasis in the early measures occurs on a closed vowel sound (''lu'') and the last unaccented tone coincides with an open sound (''jah'') as in Hál-lĕ-lú-jäh. Here the singers must take special care to stress the accented syllable and avoid emphasizing the final tone.

EX. 27   Handel, *Messiah,* ''Hallelujah Chorus''

Sometimes, though, a conflict exists between the text and the music. The solution then depends upon the context. Usually the phrasing of the music is the most flexible element. In these cases the natural emphasis of the text should predominate. At other times the accent patterns of the text and music are simply irreconcilable. The choice in such cases must always be with the music.

This shift in emphasis often happens at the end of sequences, for the focus of attention then shifts naturally from the melody and text to the points of resolution created by the harmonic and metric framework. Such a shift in emphasis occurs at the end of example 27 above, and also at the end of the Schubert ''Kyrie'' (example 28). Here the focal points of the melody should be centered upon the accented syllables of the text in the initial

EX. 28 Schubert, *Mass in G Major,* "Kyrie"

melodic sequences, and then shifted to the final harmonic resolution (despite the weak syllable—e-lei-*son*—that occurs at this point in the music).

The same strategy can be used in the excerpt from Pergolesi's *Magnificat* (example 29). Here the first expansive phrases of the melody should be shaped according to the normal accentuation of the words. But at key points within the structure—in the middle of measure 53 where the harmonic motion focuses strongly upon the dominant of the key, and at the downbeat of measure 57 where the subject returns—the thrust should be shifted to the harmonic-metric resolutions. Like many of the phrasings described earlier, this kind of shaping sets up a pattern of suppressed thrust

EX. 29 Pergolesi, *Magnificat*

EX. 29 (continued)

and eventual release that reinforces the momentum of the higher-level sequences.

REINFORCING THE MUSICAL IMPULSE

The concept of the musical phrase, we have said, is based upon the principle of the dynamic curve. Tonal actions normally begin with a growth phase of increasing energy, reach a focal point of highest intensity, and end with a concluding release. This entire sequence must be based upon a continuous flow of energy that extends through each note of the phrase to culminate in its own natural point of arrival and resolution.

The most crucial spot in this pattern is that which occurs just *before* the moment of resolution, for this is the point of highest tension, and it is the moment when a loss of intensity can have the most unfortunate effect. The situation is complicated by the fact that a change of articulation or a wide intervalic leap often separates the anacrusis and its release. In example 30 the thrust of the anacrusis must ultimately extend over the length of two octaves with no loss of intensity.

A similar pattern occurs in example 31, a theme from Debussy's *L'Après-midi d'un Faune.* In these instances the performer must not hurry the tone preceding the release. Instead, he must take care to sustain its full value and intensity to the last possible moment, so as to fully prepare for the climactic impact on the focal point of the phrase.

EX. 30 Mahler, *Symphony No. 5*, Adagietto

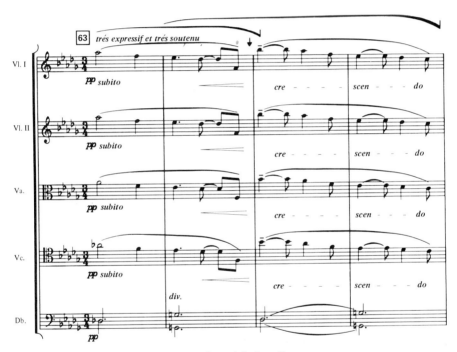

EX. 31 Debussy, *Prélude à L'Après-midi d'un Faune*

The same principle applies to phrases that contain a suppressed anacrusis or release. In example 32, the tonal thrust must seem to move into and through the downbeat, even though the projected resolution never really arrives.

In example 33, the tonal momentum must move through the rest in measure 25 into the downbeat of measure 26, for only then is the dynamic form of the sequence fully effective.[4]

---

[4] The thrust of this rest can be enhanced by playing the fortissimo chord slightly early and very abruptly; and the downbeat forte-piano slightly later than anticipated.

EX. 32 Beethoven, *Piano Sonata in E♭ Major,* Op. 7, 2nd mvt.

EX. 33 Beethoven, *String Quartet in C Minor,* Op. 18 No. 4, 1st mvt.

The most *sensitive* spot in any phrase occurs at the end of its motion, after its primary thrust has been fulfilled. It is particularly easy to neglect these points of declining energy in anticipation of the forthcoming phrase, but abrupt treatment can negate the effects of earlier shaping efforts. It can also reflect a lack of that care and concern for detail which is an essential part of every effective performance. In example 34 the first violinist must gently release bow pressure and retard bow speed on the final eighth notes, so as to carefully taper the end of each impulse.

EX. 34   Schumann, *String Quartet in A Major,* 2nd mvt.

A careful handling of phrase endings is especially important when a reserve of energy has been built up through earlier rhythmic and melodic developments. In the theme from Mozart's *Symphony No. 40* in example 35, for instance, care must be taken that the last note of each impulse remains unaccented despite its prominent tonal position.

EX. 35 Mozart, *Symphony No. 40 in G Minor,* 1st mvt.

In example 36, too, the last tone of the phrase receives a natural emphasis by virtue of its high tonal position. Any dynamic reinforcement here would detract from the classical simplicity and balanced proportions of the musical structure.

EX. 36 Mozart, *Piano Concerto in C Major,* K. 503, 1st mvt.

In example 37, from Beethoven's Sonata Op. 49 No. 1, care must be taken to lighten up on the *first* tones of the phrase, for these notes, too, receive a natural emphasis by virtue of their tonal and metric position. Indeed, the performer must gauge the perceptual weight of *every* tone so that he can meld them into the overall evolution of the sequence.[5]

[5] Each of these phrases might, of course, be shaped with equal stress on all points of emphasis, but this kind of equal accentuation, whether it occurs on every note, every beat, or every downbeat, produces a stagnation that tends to inhibit the momentum of the musical impulse. It is the principle of the dynamic curve—the sense of purposeful movement toward and away from specific points of reference *on every level of organization*—that produces the most effective musical results.

Reinforcing the dynamic form of the phrase by varying: 1 'loudness,' 2 Pace, 3 Resonance, 4 Vibrato, and 5 Duration
(volume) (tempo) (Primary)) (secondary))

EX. 37 Beethoven, *Piano Sonata in G Minor,* Op. 49 No. 1, 1st mvt.

Secondary Forms of Reinforcement

loudness + Pace
Timbre & Pitch

All of the variable elements of the music should be used to reinforce the dynamic form of the phrase.) The most basic of these, of course, are loudness and pace.) The most direct way to reinforce the shape of a phrase is with a simple increase and decrease of volume and/or tempo.)

Other forms of reinforcement, such as increased resonance, vibrato, and duration are also effective in enhancing the dynamic form of a progression.) These ''secondary'' forms of emphasis are particularly useful in reinforcing the focal points of suppressed dynamic tendencies.) For instance, a slight lengthening of the quarter note in measure 4 of example 38 can effectively enhance the significance of this tone without unduly adding to its tonal weight.

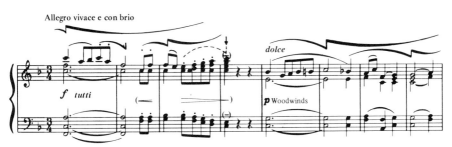

EX. 38 Beethoven, *Symphony No. 8,* 1st mvt.

The same technique can be applied to example 39A, a melody from Mozart's *Eine Kleine Nachtmusik.* Here the principal accent should be placed on the second downbeat of the phrase rather than the last tone, in order to create a suppressed dynamic tendency that can be exploited later in the piece.

This . . .

not this . . .

EX. 39A   Mozart, *Eine Kleine Nachtmusik,* 1st mvt.

The gentle reinforcement of this tone through a subtle increase of duration and resonance adds grace and beauty to the performance (example 39B). These secondary forms of accentuation should be an important part of every performer's expressive repertoire.

EX. 39B

THE DYNAMIC EQUILIBRIUM   *Balance of tension and energy.*

It is important to remember, however, that the phrasing of a composition must always be geared to the amount of tension that is generated from within its musical structure, for it is the *balanced* proportion of tension and energy that is the critical expressive factor. Each phrase must have just the

Great art & music
1 Qualities of Skill   4 Significant
2 Sincerity
3 Beauty

right momentum, each focal point just the right emphasis, each resolution just the right amount of release in relation to the character of the musical action and the style of the composition.

These dynamic proportions vary from piece to piece. Some works naturally call for an exuberant, free-wheeling style. Others require a more restrained approach. In either case an overemphasis in one direction or the other inevitably lessens the significance of the performance.

Too much control without enthusiasm seems sterile and lifeless. In such cases the structural features of the composition seem to inhibit the musical thrust. These performances seem dull, mechanical, and uninspired. On the other hand, overly energetic performances seem inconsequential, for the impulses do not seem to fit the situation. No matter how well-intentioned, excess energy is simply wasted effort.

The tremendous vitality and vibrancy of great performances comes not from energy alone, but from *focused* energy, from a clearly defined dynamic impulse that is confidently guided and shaped to the specific circumstances of a particular musical structure. In such performances, the musical energy seems contained within the musical structure but not controlled by it; its thrust is appropriate to the tonal circumstances but is not intimidated by them. Those performances radiate the qualities of skill, sincerity, beauty, and significance that have always distinguished great art and music.

Obviously the personality of the performer will influence the character of his performance. His past experience and attitudes will affect his view of this expressive balance. His playing will reveal his philosophy as well as his ability. It will reflect his understanding of human nature as well as his knowledge of musical concepts and techniques. Enthusiasm balanced with care.

But whatever his particular viewpoint, the performer must try to find that balance of enthusiasm and care that will most effectively support the character of the composition as it is contained within the musical score. He must develop the musical line in a manner that will make the piece seem to evolve naturally, its progress prepared but not predetermined, understandable but not predictable. Performances should be dominated neither by the impatience of youth nor by the measured caution of old age; neither by passion alone nor by regimented restrictions. They should strike a balance that captures just the right blend of vigor and understanding, passion and experience. Such performances reflect the fundamental qualities of significant human endeavors, and reveal the essential nature of serious, complex, rewarding human experiences.

Enthusiasm   Care
Vigor   Understanding
passion   Experience

CHAPTER 3

Patterns of Evolution

The dynamic form of a musical progression is the result of four factors:
1. The Melodic Contour
2. The Harmonic Structure
3. The Rhythmic Pattern
4. The Metric Relationship

As we have seen, the dynamic form of a musical progression is the result of a number of different factors. The melodic contour, the harmonic structure, the rhythmic patterns, the metric relationships—all of these play a role in establishing the internal shape of a developing musical impulse. The particular effect of each of these factors is discussed in this chapter. It should be kept in mind, however, that the effect of these elements can never really be separated from one another, that the dynamic form of a progression always depends upon the interaction of all tonal parameters.

THE BASIC MUSICAL ELEMENTS

Melody

One of the most important factors in determining the dynamic form of a phrase is the contour of the melodic line. Melodies often contain ascending or descending curves, scale lines, arpeggios, or other simple figures that create their own natural pattern of anacrusis, focal point, and release.

These patterns often occur in the background layers of the musical structure. In example 40, for instance, the background curve of the melody reaches to the high point of the phrase on the downbeat of measure 5, then falls to its final release in measure 10. Notice that here the thrusts of both the bass and treble melodies coincide at the principal focal point of the sequence.

Example 41 is based upon a pair of descending melodic lines. Here the thrust of the accompanying voice draws out each focal point and creates a pleading or yearning effect that dramatically underscores the meaning of the text. Notice that here again the thrusts of both voices coincide at the principal focal point of the progression.

EX. 40   Bach, *Little Prelude No. 6*

EX. 41   Bach, *B Minor Mass,* "Agnus Dei"

Incomplete melodic patterns often provide a clue to the dynamic form of an entire sequence. The first melodic impulse in Bach's *Invention No. 14* (example 42A), for instance, forms an incomplete arpeggio pattern. Since this potential remains unfulfilled, the release of this rising thrust should be suppressed, and the whole played as a series of separate, independent phrases.

EX. 42A   Bach, *Invention No. 14 in B♭ Major*

Later the motive is expanded to form a complete arpeggio figure. This sequence should be played as a series of complete one measure phrases (example 42B).

EX. 42B

A similar pattern of development occurs with the secondary motive of the piece. This impulse should be shaped with the accent on the first focal point of the motive rather than on the last tone, for this creates a suppressed dynamic tendency that can be exploited later in the work (example 42C).

EX. 42C

The dynamic implications of this motive are later fulfilled through an expansion of the melodic line into a more complete melodic pattern (example 42D).

EX. 42D

Both motives return *in stretto,* at the end of the work. Here the performer should develop a strong, continuous thrust that will reinforce the final cadential sequence (example 42E).

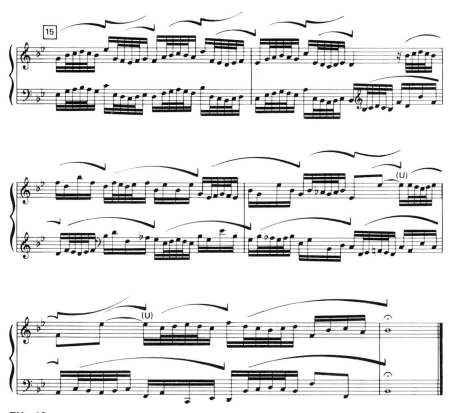

EX. 42E

Harmony

A less obvious but no less important factor in the interpretation of phrases is the harmonic structure of a progression. Harmony provides a tonal skeleton against which melodies develop, and it also creates a pattern of motion that contains its own sequence of thrusts and resolutions.

Harmonic patterns affect the dynamic evolution of a progression in different ways. On the one hand the more active, dissonant chords tend to draw attention away from less active chords, and thus carry more perceptual weight than the surrounding harmonies. In example 43, the dissonant chords on the third beats of measures 90, 92, and 96 tend to draw attention away from the surrounding chords to become the principal focal points of the phrase.

EX. 43 Tchaikowsky, *Symphony No. 6* (Pathètique), 1st mvt.

In other contexts these chords create an ongoing harmonic thrust that is ultimately focused on the final chord of resolution.) This tends to occur in more extended sequences that are based upon a ''regular'' or ''standard'' pattern of harmonic development, such as that which occurs in the middle of the last example (measures 93–95).

The same pattern of development can be seen in example 44, an abstract from Schumann's *Dichterliebe*. In this case attention is initially

EX. 44   Schumann, *Dichterliebe*, No. 1

spran-gen, da ist in mei - nem Her – zen die Lie - be auf - ge - gan-gen.

ritard.

EX. 44 (continued)

drawn to the chromatically active, inverted IV chord in measures 1 and 3. However, as the sequence develops, attention is gradually shifted toward the end of the progression. The sequence ultimately focuses on the tonic D major chord in measure 12.

Sudden, unexpected harmonic shifts often provide a critical dynamic impetus in progressions that are based upon a repeating motivic pattern. This is evident in Chopin's *Prelude in A Major* (example 45). The piece is based upon a single two-measure motive that contains little harmonic momentum. However, the suppressed forward thrust of this motive is reinforced at the climax of the piece (bar 12) by a sudden shift to an altered F♯ dominant 7th chord. This harmonic shift is maintained in the following measure, and then the piece reverts to the original pattern in the final bars.

EX. 45 Chopin, *Prelude in A Major*, Op. 28 No. 7

V^9 I V^7

I V^7 of II   II V^9 I

EX. 45 (continued)

Harmony plays a similar role in the first theme of Schubert's *Symphony No. 5* (example 46A). Here again the principal motive contains a strong melodic impetus, but little harmonic momentum.

The suppressed thrust of this motive is harmonically reinforced in the

EX. 46A Schubert, *Symphony No. 5,* 1st mvt.

second half of the progression, and the phrase is eventually extended to the final downbeat of the sequence (example 46B).

EX. 46B

Meter

The metric structure of a progression is of major importance in determining its dynamic form. Meter provides a background series of pulses of different strength, within which and against which rhythmic patterns develop. This metric framework enables the listener to time the evolution of the musical impulse and anticipate its moments of release.

Of course the focal points of a musical impulse don't always coincide with the strong beats of the metric structure. In example 47, for instance, the principal focal points of the melody are centered on the weaker, *second* beats of the measure. This creates an imbalanced, noncongruent pattern of development that enhances the dynamic intensity of the music and reinforces its forward momentum. This noncongruent pattern is resolved in the final measures of the sequence.

EX. 47 Schumann, *Kinderscenen,* Op. 15 No. 7, "Traumerei"

For the same reason, the initial motive in Chopin's B Minor Prelude (example 48A) is best shaped toward the high point of the phrase rather than the following downbeat release. In this case the emphasis can be shifted more strongly to the downbeat in each progressive statement, climaxing in the chromatic shift of harmony on the downbeat of measure 6, and repeated in the treble on the downbeats of measures 7 and 8.

EX. 48A   Chopin, *Prelude in B Minor,* Op. 28 No. 6

These shifts of emphasis are repeated in the next section of the piece (example 48B). Here they are even more obvious, since the high point itself is shifted from the second beat of the phrase in measure 9 to the downbeat of the phrase in measure 12. Similar shifts occur throughout the rest of the composition.

EX. 48B

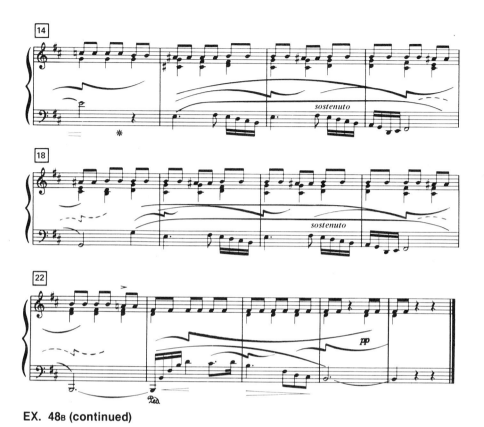

EX. 48b (continued)

A similar pattern occurs in Chopin's *Prelude in C Major* (example 49A). Here too, a strong noncongruent arpeggio pattern is played against a firm metric framework. In this case a strong secondary thrust is created by the rising sequence at the end of the motive in the soprano and tenor voices. These conflicting tendencies support the "agitato" character of the music and reinforce its forward momentum.

EX. 49a Chopin, *Prelude in C Major*, Op. 28 No. 1

The development of the motive is handled somewhat differently in this piece, for instead of being resolved at the climax of the work, the final upward thrust of the motive is inverted and forced to *conform* to the curve of the dominant arpeggio pattern. This occurs in measure 5, and again, momentarily, in measure 15, and then finally in measure 21, at the high point of the piece (example 49B).

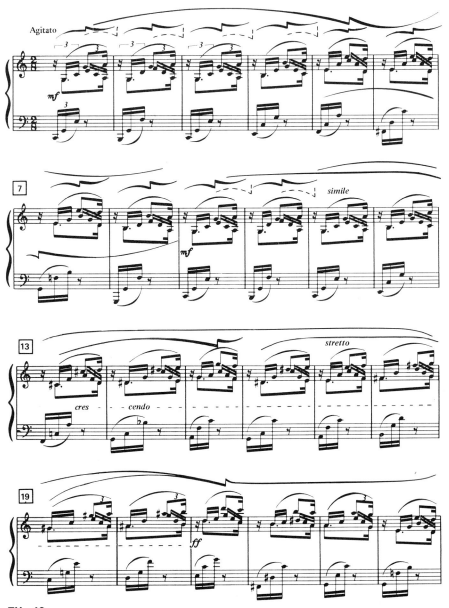

EX. 49B

But the drama is not yet complete, for the *congruent possibilities* of this motive have yet to be fulfilled. In fact it is not until the end of the piece, after a series of teasing reversals in measures 25–28, that this potential is reinforced (example 49C). It is accomplished by extending the C over the bar line and by a partial inversion of the arpeggio figure in the alto voice. These changes help to extend the thrust of the musical impulse into the following downbeats, a fact that should be reflected in the performance of the final bars of this work.

EX. 49c

SHIFTING DYNAMIC RELATIONSHIPS

The intimate relationship of rhythm and meter is particularly evident in progressions that are based upon a single motivic pattern. In example 50, for instance, the principal motive is shifted from its initial upbeat position and forced to serve as the downbeat release in the second half of the phrase, as indicated by the brackets underneath the treble staff. This shift in position gradually transforms the downbeat release in measures 1 and 3 into an

EX. 50 Brahms, *Symphony No. 3,* 3rd mvt.

EX. 50 (continued)

anacrusis, and places an unusual amount of tension on these tones in a way that reinforces the momentum of the entire theme.

In example 51A the primary motive undergoes similar shifts of position and function. In this case the interpretation depends upon subtle changes that occur in the melodic, harmonic, and rhythmic structure of the music.

The basic motive of this theme is first centered upon the downbeat of measure 1. It is then expanded in sequence to the downbeat of measure 2, and then again to the downbeat of measure 4. This last release is centered upon a rising arpeggio figure which, because of its upward momentum, creates a new secondary dynamic tendency. (This rising figure is based upon the initial upbeat motive, but here it has been shifted to a different metric position, as indicated by the brackets underneath the score.)

The motive is repeated in measure 5, but due to the chromatic alteration and harmonic changes that occur here, the primary accent of this phrase tends to shift to the last and longest note of the impulse, centered on the *second* beat of the measure. This motive is again repeated in measure 6, but now the last note has been shortened, so that the focal point of *this* phrase tends to revert *back* to the downbeat of the measure.

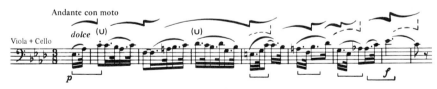

EX. 51A Beethoven, *Symphony No. 5,* 2nd mvt.

All of these conflicts are then resolved as the motive returns to its original upbeat position, just in time to climax on the sudden "forte" downbeat of measure 7. (The thrust of the *first* upbeat impulse, incidentally, should be gently suppressed because of its progressive expansion and resolution at this point.)

And so the initial upbeat motive (example 51B, bracket a) served as a downbeat release (bracket b), a noncongruent anacrusis (bracket c), another downbeat release (bracket d), and finally another upbeat anacrusis (bracket e). These shifting shapes and alternating accents provide variety in what could become a static, repetitive pattern of development.

EX. 51B

The progression is not yet completed, however. This resolution is also unstable and, being the dominant of the key, develops secondary tendencies of its own, tendencies that are expanded, reinforced, and ultimately resolved in the remaining measures of the progression (example 51C).[1]

EX. 51C

[1] The basic dynamic levels of this piece, incidentally, must also be maintained. Thus the progression begins *piano* and does not change to *forte* until the downbeat of measure 7. However, such general indications should not preclude the sensitive shaping of the internal phrase patterns. These markings indicate only the general *range* of dynamics; they do not indicate a lack of expressivity.

Alternative Patterns of Interpretation

The perception of metric structure in the kinds of pieces we have been discussing often depends upon the articulation of the rhythmic patterns of the music. The metric structure of example 52A, for instance, depends upon the grouping and accentuation of the tones. This melody is sometimes performed as if it contained a series of repeated triplet impulses.

Performed . . .

EX. 52A   Beethoven, *Symphony No. 5,* 3rd mvt.

This actually results in a change of the perceived metric structure. Although the piece is written in ³/₄, when played this way it is heard in ⁶/₈, as indicated by the metric accents underneath the score (example 52B).

Heard . . .

EX. 52B

This version is certainly easier to perform, but the progression is more effective when played as written, in ³/₄ time, for the original strongly reinforces its inherent forward momentum (example 52C).[2]

EX. 52C

[2] The key tone in this sequence is the *third* note of the measure. If this 8th note is played as an unaccented tone (in relation to the previous tone) the meter is altered, as indicated in example 52B. However, if it is slightly emphasized as in example 52C, the meter remains unchanged, despite the fact that the *fourth* tone of the measure receives a natural accent by virtue of its prominent tonal position.

EX. 52 (continued)

A similar situation occurs in Von Einem's piano piece, example 53A.

EX. 53A Von Einem, *Four Piano Pieces*, No. 4 (*Copyright 1944 by Universal Edition, Wien. Used by permission of European American Music Distribution Corporation, sole U.S. agent for Universal Edition.*)

EX. 53A (continued)

Here, too, the rhythm might be performed as a series of triplet (and duplet) impulses (example 53B).

EX. 53B

However, it is more effective when played as written, as a series of syncopated rhythms in 2/2 time (example 53C).

EX. 53C

This phrasing is especially important here since the dynamic form of the piece depends upon a shift of the meter from the original 2/2 to the later 3/8 time. When played this way the syncopated patterns of the earlier measures are "resolved" by a shift to the more regular 3/8 meter at the climax of the piece, in bar 24 (example 53D).

The same principle applies to the following Bartok excerpts. In example 54 the tones should be *grouped* according to the beaming of the notes, but they should be *accented* according to the notated metric structure.

EX. 53ᴅ

Otherwise the syncopations will be lost and the progression will sound as if it were written in a meter different from the one indicated in the score.

This . . .

EX. 54 Bartok, *Mikrokosmos,* Syncopation, No. 133, Vol. V (*Copyright 1940 by Hawkes & Son (London) Ltd, renewed 1967. Reprinted by permission of Boosey & Hawkes, Inc.*)

not this . . .

EX. 54 (continued)

On the other hand, example 55, taken from the same work, should be phrased according to its irregular metric structure *and* its beamed tones.

EX. 55   Bartok, *Mikrokosmos,* Dance in Bulgarian Rhythm, No. 151, Vol. VI

STYLE

Irregular, noncongruent rhythmic patterns often create a strong perceptual expectation of resolution and a return to more balanced patterns of motion. However, such conflicts are not always resolved. Especially in Classical and Neoclassical music, certain noncongruent cross-relationships may be maintained throughout an entire composition. In the Mozart melody of example 56, for instance, a consistent relationship is maintained between the natural emphasis of the downbeat and the internal phrase accents that are centered on the third beat of each measure, and no effort is made to resolve this noncongruent pattern.

EX. 56 Mozart, *String Quartet in G Major,* K. 387, 1st mvt.

The same is true of example 57, from Bach's *Brandenburg Concerto No. 2.* Here the thrust of each impulse is centered upon the weaker, second downbeat of each two-measure unit, and this basic noncongruent relationship is maintained throughout the piece.

Similar dynamic forms occur in more romantic styles of music, although here the internal conflicts have a stronger tendency to resolve on the higher levels of the musical structure. Yet here too, their ultimate disposition depends upon the overall character of the piece, for these internal cross-relationships always have two primary functions. On the one hand they serve to enhance the dynamic intensity and emotional tone of the music; on the other hand they serve to reinforce the ongoing momentum of

EX. 57 Bach, *Brandenburg Concerto No. 2,* 3rd mvt.

the higher-level musical impulses. And although one or the other of these functions may predominate in any particular composition, the balanced relationship of *both* functions is an essential aspect of every musical performance.

The Musical Context

Other stylistic factors also affect the phrasing and interpretation of compositions. It is sometimes necessary, for instance, to suppress the reinforcement of *any* dynamic pattern in consideration of a composition's basic mood or emotional tone. Certain Impressionistic works, for example, call for a deemphasis on all levels of motion. Other ''misterioso'' pieces and certain introductory patterns call for a similar dynamic restraint.[3]

Certain other pieces—marches and dances, for instance—require a strong, consistent emphasis on the lower levels of the musical structure.

[3] See the excerpts from Beethoven's 4th Symphony in example 26, Beethoven's 9th Symphony in example 67, and Brahms' 3rd Symphony in example 116.

The stately, majestic character of Rimsky-Korsakov's sultan theme in example 7 and the melody from the *New World Symphony* in example 9 are enhanced by a firm, consistent support of their recurring rhythmic patterns. The same is true of finales, codas, and repeated cadential resolutions. Here it is better to accentuate the lower-level impulses so as to insure the release of all accumulated tensions.

A careful shaping of higher-level patterns is often also inappropriate in the country tunes and folk melodies encountered in such composers as Haydn, Bartok, and Mahler. Here it is precisely the *absence* of carefully balanced phrasing that gives them their carefree character. These melodies should not be played in a serious manner, for it is their uninhibited bursts of energy—the feeling of doing something just for the fun of it—that reinforces their exuberant, free-spirited quality.

The same kind of excess energy, stretched to exaggerated proportions, can add a humorous touch to a melody. The musical joke in the second movement of Haydn's "Surprise" Symphony (example 58), for instance, is not simply a result of the sudden accent, for many pieces contain such subito over–emphases. The joke lies in the fact that the musical context does not call for, and the tonal structure cannot support, such a forceful impact. The fortissimo accent is therefore inappropriate in this context.

EX. 58   Haydn, *Symphony No. 94* ("Surprise"), 2nd mvt.

The same is true of the suppressed resolution in Haydn's minuet (example 59) as compared to the suppressed resolution from the *Eroica Symphony* (example 60). Haydn is obviously kidding us here, whereas Beethoven is perfectly serious.

EX. 59 Haydn, *Symphony No. 104*, 3rd mvt.

EX. 60 Beethoven, *Symphony No. 3* (Eroica), 1st mvt.

Conversely, one of the reasons popularized versions of classical themes often seem offensive is that these performances ignore their dynamic structure in favor of a blatant reinforcement of all musical accents, regardless of their meaning or significance. Such a breach of etiquette is not a moral issue, but these caricatures should not be confused with serious art.

Mussorgsky's "In the Village"

These contrasts in style are evident in the following excerpts, taken from Mussorgsky's *In the Village*. The theme of this work is first presented in the style of a fantasia. Here the character of the music calls for a gentle, freely expressive treatment (example 61A).

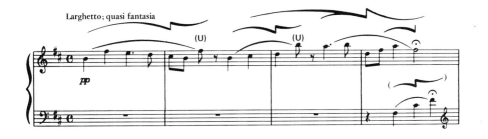

EX. 61A Mussorgsky, *In the Village*

In the first variation (example 61B), the same melody is presented as a march. Here the regularity of the meter is of primary importance, and here too the lower levels of the musical structure should predominate. In this case a careful, sensitive treatment of the phrases would be entirely out of place.

EX. 61B

In the next sections of the piece (example 61C), the melody is used as the basis of a scherzo, and then as a gypsy melody. Here again delicate phrasing would be inappropriate. In fact, the sensitive tones that would be carefully treated in other contexts now become the "butt" of syncopated accents and other "impertinent" developments. These accents add a joyous, carefree character to the music.

EX. 61c

If he wishes to engage in a serious interpretive effort, the performer must take into account *all* of the factors that affect the expressive tone and dynamic impact of a composition. Above all, he must try to arrive at an interpretation that reinforces the essential character and spirit of the music as it is contained within its particular dynamic structure.) Anything less is a disservice to the composer.)

CHAPTER 4

Rhythm and Meter

The relationship of rhythm and meter, we have seen, is a primary source of musical intensity and momentum. Indeed, the interaction between these two elements is a key factor in the dynamic evolution of most musical sequences. This relationship often involves a fundamental conflict that is exploited in the early stages of a progression and then resolved at the completion of the sequence.

In example 62 (originally analyzed in example 47), we saw how a series of noncongruent phrases created an imbalanced pattern of develop-

EX. 62 Schumann, *Kinderscenen,* Op. 15 No. 7, "Traumerei"

ment that is resolved later in the progression. Here the principal focal points of the phrase are initially centered on the weaker, second beats of the measure. The focal point is then shifted to the stronger downbeat position at the end of the sequence.)

HIGHER-LEVEL STRUCTURES

Similar patterns of development occur on the higher levels of the musical structure. For instance, example 63A is written in cut-time. Its measures, however, are also grouped by the listener into hypermetric units of two measures each, as indicated by the metric accents below the staff.

EX. 63A   Schubert, *Symphony No. 5*, 1st mvt.

√The melody in this example, you will recall, is based upon a beginning-accented motive that contains a suppressed dynamic tendency which is harmonically reinforced in the second half of the progression. This shift resolves the initial conflict, but it also creates a new pattern of imbalance, since these motives are now centered on the weaker, *second* downbeat of each two-measure unit)(example 63B).

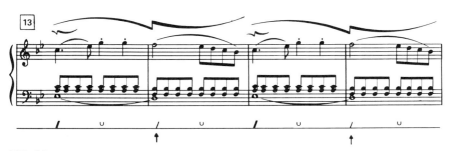

EX. 63B

This *hypermetric* noncongruence is resolved by an extension of the melody in the final phrase of the progression (example 63C).

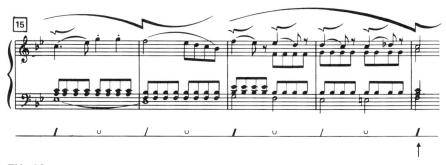

EX. 63c

A similar pattern of development occurs in the next song by Hugo Wolf (example 64A). This piece is written in 2/4 time, and here too, the measures are perceptually grouped into hypermeasures of two bars each.

EX. 64A Wolf, "Das Verlassene Mägdlein," from *Gedichte von Mörike*

The introductory notes of this song might be grouped in terms of a beginning-accented motive, as in example 64B, or an end-accented motive, as in example 64C.

Either this . . .

EX. 64B

or this . . .

EX. 64C

Here the first interpretation is best, and in fact Wolf specifies this interpretation by his phrasing of the first four bars of the music (example 64D).

EX. 64ᴅ (Composer's edition)

The suppressed tendencies of this motive are reinforced in the vocal line beginning in measure 5 (example 64E).[2] This shift in emphasis resolves the first conflict but creates a new hypermetric noncongruence, just as in the previous Schubert excerpt.

EX. 64ᴇ

[1] Tempo is a crucial factor here, for if this introduction is taken too fast, the *second* phrasing automatically predominates.

[2] Significantly, Wolf discontinues the phrase-lines at this point, for here the accompaniment should reinforce the phrasing in the vocal line.

This pattern is repeated throughout the first two verses of the song and then it is expanded again, into a four measure, congruent phrase at the (suppressed) climax of the composition (example 64F).

EX. 64F

The first verse of the song is then repeated, but with an important alteration; the final phrase in the voice part is delayed for one measure so that its focal point may coincide with a primary hypermetric pulse (example 64G).

This same principle played an important role in our interpretation of the final measures of Chopin's *Prelude in C Major,* originally analyzed in example 49. Here the final phrase is centered upon the penultimate, rather than the final downbeat, primarily because this is the final hypermetric pulse (example 65).

EX. 65 Chopin, *Prelude in C Major,* Op. 28 No. 1

Other Hypermetric Patterns of Development

Like their lower-level counterparts, the upper-level conflicts are not always resolved. In example 66 the thrust of the final phrase, like that of the earlier phrases, is centered upon a weaker hypermetric pulse. This kind of patterning rounds out the musical action and tends to produce closed or sectional musical forms.

EX. 66   Beethoven, *Piano Sonata in G Minor,* Op. 49 No. 1, 1st mvt.

At other times the *hypermetric* patterns are altered to coincide with the *rhythmic* structure of the music. The melody in example 67A contains a potential thrust that is tentatively focused on the fourth downbeat of every four-measure unit.

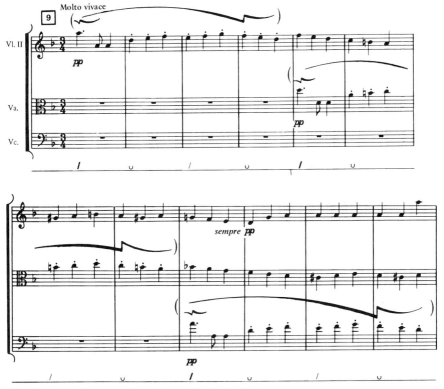

EX. 67A   Beethoven, *Symphony No. 9,* 2nd mvt.

Later this thrust is reinforced by a shift to triple hypermetric group-ings (example 67B).

EX. 67B

Eventually the momentum of the entire movement is resolved by shifting to a duple metric pattern on both levels of organization (example 67C).

Pivotal Metric Shifts

Metric shifts such as those discussed are often created by a change in the function of a single hypermetric pulse. In example 68 the strong harmonic and rhythmic sequence that occurs just before measure 16 causes

EX. 67c

EX. 68 Beethoven, *Piano Concerto No. 1,* 1st mvt.

EX. 68 (continued)

the downbeat of measure 15 to serve a dual function in the progression, in much the same way that a chord serves a dual function in a pivotal tonal modulation. (This pivotal metric function is indicated by the symbol Ʋ below the staff.) The metric shift enhances the continuity of the entire sequence.

A similar pattern of development occurs in example 69A. Here, too, the primary motive has strong, suppressed tendencies that are focused on the weaker, second downbeat of each two-measure unit.

EX. 69A   Bach, *Invention No. 4 in D Minor*

This conflict is resolved once during the course of the piece and twice in succession at the end of the work, through a shift in metric structure and an extension of the motivic impulse (example 69B). These shifts enhance the thrust of the cadential statements and should be reflected in the performance of the final measures of the piece.

EX. 69B

Similar metric shifts are evident in example 70A, from Tchaikowsky's *Symphony No. 4* in F Minor. As we saw earlier, the suppressed tendencies of the principal motive (measures 1–4) are eventually reinforced in the second half of the theme (measures 13–20). However, this creates a new conflict since the focal points are now centered on a weaker hypermetric pulse.

EX. 70A   Tchaikowsky, *Symphony No. 4,* 2nd mvt.

EX. 70A (continued)

When this motive returns after the middle section of the movement, it is shifted to a new hypermetric position. This adjustment reinforces the suppressed thrust of the motive, and enhances the momentum of the entire sequence (example 70B).

EX. 70B

EX. 70B (continued)

At the close of the movement the motive returns in its original position, but then the *hypermetric structure* is shifted to offset this change. This metric shift again reinforces the forward thrust of the motive and sets the stage for a series of gentle congruent impulses that serve to resolve the conflicts that were developed earlier in the movement (example 70C).

EX. 70C

Tempo

The tempo of the music directly affects the perception of these hypermetric patterns. This is evident in a comparison of two similar Beethoven themes, illustrated in examples 71 and 72. Both of these melodies begin with a rising impulse whose thrust is focused on the second downbeat of the phrase. Because of its faster tempo, example 71 contains a strong sense of hypermetric noncongruence, a conflict that is forcefully resolved on the downbeat of measure 7.

EX. 71   Beethoven, *Piano Sonata in F Minor,* Op. 2 No. 1, 1st mvt.

The phrases of example 72, on the other hand, are already focused upon the primary downbeats of the metric structure, so this progression contains no significant higher-level conflicts.

EX. 72   Beethoven, *Piano Sonata in A Major,* Op. 2 No. 2, 3rd mvt.

EX. 72 (continued)

AMBIGUOUS METRIC STRUCTURES

The situation is complicated by the fact that the hypermetric structure of a composition isn't always clear at the beginning of a work. In example 73, the initial harmonic ambiguity and the syncopation serve to establish the downbeat of the *second* measure as the primary hypermetric pulse. Here the entire first measure serves as a single hypermetric upbeat.

EX. 73 Ravel, *Valses Nobles et Sentimentales*, No. VII (*Copyright 1912 Durand S. A. Used by permission of the agent, Theodore Presser Company*).

The situation is even less clear in the next example. Because of the strong melodic thrust that is focused on the downbeat of the second measure, this piece, too, might be performed as if it began with a hypermetric upbeat (example 74A).

EX. 74A   Mozart, *Piano Sonata in D Major,* K. 576, 1st mvt.

If, however, the first downbeat is gently accented, an entirely different pattern emerges (example 74B). The first interpretation of this progression is simpler and more regular, but the second is preferable since it creates a variety of imbalances that can be exploited later in the movement.

EX. 74B

Similar hypermetric ambiguity is common in developmental and transitional sections, where it becomes, in a sense, the metric analogue of those modulating sequences that have no clearly-established tonal center. This is evident in the following excerpt from the minuet of Mozart's G Minor Symphony. The hypermetric patterns of this movement begin with a triple grouping of measures that contains a strong noncongruent melodic thrust (example 75A).

EX. 75A   Mozart, *Symphony No. 40 in G Minor,* 3rd mvt.

This conflict is tentatively resolved on the downbeat of measure 9, but then the music moves through a modulating sequence that tends to weaken the hypermetric groupings (example 75B).

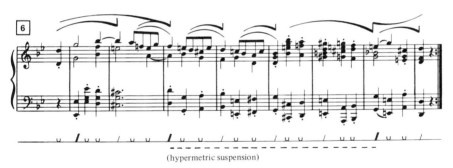

(hypermetric suspension)

EX. 75B

The initial patterns return in the second section of the minuet, enhanced by the contrapuntal line in the violins. This is followed by an even longer hypermetric suspension and, ultimately, by a return to a more stable metric framework (example 75C).

Because of the absence of any clear-cut higher-level patterns, the musical momentum can bog down in these transition sections. This tendency can be offset by a continual pressing on of the musical impulse. In each case the tonal thrust must continue to move firmly into and through the final downbeat release.

EX. 75c

Ambiguous Lower-Level Structures

Ambiguous metric patterns sometimes also occur on the lower levels of the metric structure. For example, the metric structure of the fugue subject in example 76A has a rather ambivalent character and could be shaped in either of two ways.

Either this . . .

or this. . .

EX. 76A   Bach, *Fugue in D Major*

The piece begins with the first version (example 76B) but soon incorporates the second version as well (example 76C).

EX. 76B

EX. 76C

EX. 76c (continued)

Because of this metric ambivalence, it is important to establish the metric structure of the piece at the outset; otherwise the form of the opening measures will be unclear and the dynamic shape of the piece will be less effective.[3]

The same is true of the following excerpt from Beethoven's C Major Piano Concerto (example 77A).

EX. 77A   Beethoven, *Piano Concerto No. 1,* 3rd mvt.

Because the normal pattern of 8th and 16th notes is reversed, the initial motive in this sequence might be heard with the accent on the first rather than the second tone. This shift in rhythmic emphasis tends to alter the underlying metric patterns as well (example 77B).

EX. 77B

Such metric distortion is inappropriate here. Although the movement is filled with humor, a change in the notated meter (and the resulting metric shift four bars later) disturbs the driving "rondo" character of the piece.

[3] Even in the unlikely event that it was intended by the composer, such lower-level metric ambiguity will not be accepted by the mind of the listener. It is a well-established fact that the mind reflexively tries to organize ambiguous perceptual structures, and in this case it automatically latches on to one or the other alternative. The question here is whether or not this reflexive mental organization should be controlled, or simply left to chance.

Alternative Patterns of Interpretation

Of course there are situations where the notated meter is not the one that is heard by the listener, nor the one that *should* be heard by the listener. In the following Brahms *Intermezzo* (example 78), for instance, the listener is intentionally led to believe that the beat is where it isn't. The appearance of the theme therefore brings with it a shock of recognition as to the actual position of the metric structure.

EX. 78   Brahms, *Intermezzo,* Op. 10 No. 3

The third movement of Schumann's Piano Concerto (example 79A) provides another instance of a meter that is seen but not heard. Listeners who watch the conductor or musicians who are familiar with the score may mentally impose a duple pattern here, but the rhythm itself creates a simple ³/₂ meter.

Notated . . .

EX. 79A   Schumann, *Piano Concerto in A Minor,* 3rd mvt.

Heard . . .

EX. 79B

It would also be wrong to try to force the theme of Mozart's *Sonata in C Major* into the notated metric structure (example 80A). Such a performance would distort the simple, straightforward character of the piece.

Notated . . .

EX. 80A   Mozart, *Piano Sonata in C Major*, K. 545, 3rd mvt.

Heard . . .

EX. 80B

It would be simpler, of course, if the performer could always rely upon the printed score to clear up any ambiguities of interpretation. Unfortunately this is not possible. Music notation is an inexact system developed over hundreds of years by many different individuals. Often the scores themselves have undergone considerable editing and revision.

In any case, the performer must remember that the printed score is only an approximate representation of the music as it was originally conceived in the mind of the composer. It is the primary responsibility of the performer to interpret that score with as much insight, skill, and understanding as he can muster.

CHAPTER 5

Rubato

One of the most useful means available to the performer for the shaping of phrases is *rubato*. This technique, which is based upon subtle readjustments in the timing of the rhythmic patterns directly reinforces the amount of tension that is generated from within the musical impulse.)

Most musical resolutions tend to coincide with the strong beats of the metric structure. A slight ritard before the arrival of these metric pulses tends to increase the level of musical tension and so produces a stronger resolution when the release finally does occur.

However, these ritards can inhibit the momentum of the higher-level actions. As a result, the beginning of the phrase is normally accelerated, producing a continuous ebb-and-flow effect that does not greatly disturb the hypermetric proportions. This initial accelerando also enhances the forward momentum of the phrase so that its thrust is reinforced at both ends of its development.

These effects are illustrated in the excerpt from Chopin's *Prelude in E Minor* (example 81). Here an arrow (→) indicates a subtle increase in tempo, and a wavy line (⌇) indicates a slight rubato ritard.

EX. 81 Chopin, *Prelude in E Minor,* Op. 28 No. 4

Rubato technique is also effective in enhancing the thrust of suppressed, secondary dynamic tendencies.) In example 82 a slight ritard just before the second downbeat draws attention to this suppressed resolution without the use of additional tonal reinforcement.

EX. 82 Schumann, *Dichterliebe,* No. 1

Rubato shadings must be used with restraint, and always in proportion to the higher-level patterns of development. This is indicated in examples 83 and 84, which are harmonic-metric abstracts of the two previous
compositions.[1]

EX. 83 Abstract, Chopin, *Prelude in E Minor*

[1]Talking to one of his students, Chopin used a candle to illustrate his concept of
rubato. "This is my rubato," he said, blowing gently at the flame. "This is your rubato,"
he said, and blew out the candle.

EX. 83 (continued)

EX. 84 Abstract, Schumann, *Dichterliebe,* No. 1 (Originally analyzed in Ex. 44.)

EX. 84 (continued)

LOWER-LEVEL PATTERNS

Rubato adjustments can occur over the span of several beats, or they can happen within the space of a single pulse. For example, the insertion of a sudden, momentary pause just before the arrival of a strong downbeat resolution can significantly increase the force of its impact. Used in conjunction with an interruption in the flow of sound, these slight "luftpause" delays (indicated by the sign v in the examples) can enhance the dynamic effect of the entire progression. (Notice, incidentally, how the use of this technique in example 85 produces a physical lift of the bow that results in a natural accent on the return impact.)

EX. 85 Mahler, *Symphony No. 1,* 2nd mvt.

103

The same technique can be used in the scherzo from Beethoven's *Eroica Symphony* (example 86). Here several sforzando accents occur in what is otherwise a rather simple context. A slight luftpause just before the principal releases reinforces the thrust of the impulse and enhances the significance of the resolutions. (Notice that here, too, the delay produces an increase in the horn player's store of diaphragmatic tension, and so makes the sforzando easier to play.)

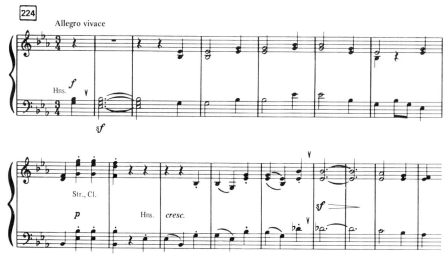

EX. 86 Beethoven, *Symphony No. 3 (Eroica)*, 3rd mvt.

In example 87, a luftpause helps to mark the beginning of a new phrase.

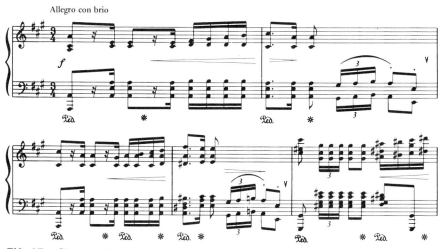

EX. 87 Chopin, *Polonaise No. 3*, Op. 40 No. 1

The Dual Rhythmic Functions

These luftpause delays, however, are useful only in special circumstances.) They can be used effectively only when the tones involved delineate the strong metric subdivisions of the music.) This has been demonstrated by experiments that were designed to measure normal performance procedures.) These experiments have revealed that tones which do *not* articulate strong metric subdivisions tend to be placed *closer* to the beat than the strict mathematical proportions of the music would normally indicate.) For example, in the progression in example 88A, the 16th-note thrusts of each motive tend to be placed closer to the following half-note release than notated.

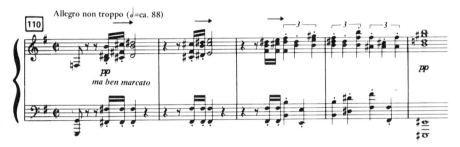

EX. 88A   Brahms, *Symphony No. 4,* 1st mvt.

Tones that articulate strong metric subdivisions are *not* so displaced.) The quarter-note upbeats in example 88B, for instance, tend to maintain their notated metric position, and in fact are often *separated* from the downbeat release by a slight luftpause delay.

EX. 88B

Another illustration of this principle can be found in the Mendelssohn theme in example 89. Here the eighth notes in measures 378 and 380 must remain close to the following downbeats despite the rubato ritard at the end of the measure. But when the motive returns in altered form in measure 384 the new quarter-note upbeat must coincide *with* the rubato ritard.

105

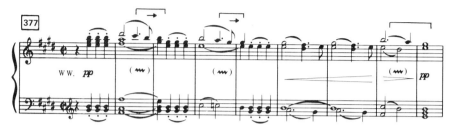

EX. 89 Mendelssohn, *Violin Concerto in E Minor,* 1st mvt.

The reason for this difference lies in the intimate relationship of rhythm and meter. Since rubato alterations normally affect the metric proportions, tones that articulate these metric subdivisions must coincide with changes in the placement of the beat, and so prepare for the upcoming metric resolution. But those rhythmic impulses that do *not* articulate these subdivisions remain relatively independent of the metric structure and so may be used to enhance the rhythmic thrust of the music.

The foregoing functions are particularly evident in the following Beethoven theme (example 90). This melody is based upon a series of short 32nd-note *rhythmic anticipations* whose impulsive thrusts, when placed very near the following release, strongly enhance the tensive qualities of the music. However, this pattern suddenly changes into a series of eighth note *metric upbeats* at the high point of the melody. These eighth notes, played with strict metric regularity, help to prepare for the climax of the theme in measure 4.

EX. 90 Beethoven, *Piano Sonata in C Minor (Pathètique),* Op. 13, 1st mvt.

A similar pattern occurs in Mozart's Overture to *The Magic Flute* (example 91). Here it is best to play the initial 16th- and 32nd-note figures as short, thrusting rhythmic anticipations, and place them closer to their point of release than the notated rhythm would normally indicate. These abrupt rhythmic thrusts, along with the following sforzando overemphases and syncopations, establish a reserve of inhibited tension and energy that helps to fuel the pulsating rhythms and melodies of the following Allegro section. (The 16th-note patterns in measures 5 and 7, on the other hand, must maintain their notated metric position.)

EX. 91 Mozart, *The Magic Flute*, Overture

Double-Dotted Rhythms

The distinction between the rhythmic anticipation and the metric upbeat is especially important in introductory and concluding passages, for then the particular function of each pattern is especially apparent. In fact, this distinction serves as the basis for a rather unusual performance practice, as illustrated in example 92 from Handel's *Messiah*. In the introductory passages of the musical form known as the French Overture, the rhythmic patterns are normally played as double-dotted, rather than as the notated single-dotted pattern. According to C.P.E. Bach, "[In these contexts] the short notes following dotted notes are always performed shorter than their notation requires."[2]

Notated . . .

EX. 92A   Handel, *Messiah,* Overture

Performed . . .

EX. 92B

The psychological basis for this practice seems clear. In the slow introductions of these works the conclusive character of the strong upbeat-release pattern would be out of place, whereas the impulsive thrust of the rhythmic anticipation helps to set the stage for the Allegro section that

---

[2] This quote and others in this chapter are taken principally from Robert Donington, *A Performer's Guide to Baroque Music* (New York: Charles Scribner's Sons, 1974), and from his *The Interpretation of Early Music* (New York: St. Martin's Press, Inc., 1963).

follows, just as in the Overture to *The Magic Flute.* Leopold Mozart, for example, felt that the single–dotted rhythms sounded "sleepy" and, along with many other authorities, recommended the use of the double-dotted pattern in these contexts.

Final cadences, though, are a different matter. Here the release of accumulated tension is accomplished more effectively by the stronger upbeat pattern. Thus in the final measures of the *Messiah* Overture, the notated single-dotted rhythm is more appropriate, and should be used here to provide a more satisfying conclusion to the movement (example 92C).

Played as written . . .

EX. 92c

The conclusive effect of the upbeat-release pattern is so important that its use is appropriate even in double-dotted contexts. This situation occurs at the end of the first movement of Franck's *D Minor Symphony* (example 93). Here the quarter note upbeats of the primary motive (measures 513–517) are transformed into anticipatory, double-dotted rhythms (measures 517 and 519), mirroring a change that occurred at the beginning of the first theme. This change in function is reinforced by the fact that, contrary to normal procedure, *no* ritard is indicated in these final measures.

And yet even here a slight tenuto on these eighth note anticipations is not out of character, for it helps to seal the thrust of the final rhythmic impulses, and it reinforces the resolution of the entire movement.[3]

[3]The duration of a rhythmic anticipation can also be lengthened somewhat just before the focal point of a phrase. A subtle expansion of the last note in measure 2 of the *Messiah* Overture, for instance, reinforces the climactic point of the phrase. The important

point here is that the exact length of these tones is flexible, and should be adjusted according to the function of the phrase and the character of the music.

EX. 93 Franck, *Symphony in D Minor,* 1st mvt.

Rhythmic Releases

The same principle applies to notes that follow strong metric pulses. For instance, in example 94A the tones of the primary motive tend to be placed *closer* to the initial pulse than the precise mathematical proportions of the music would normally indicate. Played slightly faster than notated, these impulsive figures enhance the dynamic intensity of the music.

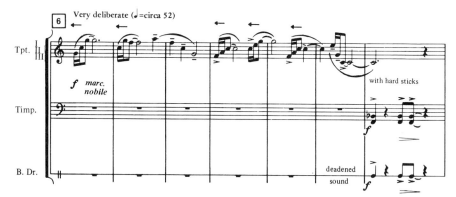

EX. 94A Copland, *Fanfare for the Common Man (Copyright 1944 by Aaron Copland, renewed 1971. Arranged by permission of Aaron Copland, copyright owner, and Boosey & Hawkes, Inc., sole publishers and licensees. Reprinted by permission of Boosey & Hawkes, Inc.)*

Later, the same rhythms reappear in augmentation. These patterns should be played in strict metric time, for such metric regularity helps to release the tension and thrust of all earlier developments (example 94B).

EX. 94B

The theme in example 95, from Beethoven's *Piano Concerto No. 1,* illustrates the same principle. Here a slight luftpause just before the downbeat, and a subtle acceleration just afterward, reinforce the dance-like quality of the music and increase its forward momentum.[4]

EX. 95 Beethoven, *Piano Concerto No. 1,* 3rd mvt.

In example 96, the combination of upbeat luftpause and downbeat accelerando produces the lilting rhythms of the Viennese waltz.

EX. 96 Strauss, *Die Fledermaus*

This technique can be used effectively in the excerpt from Ravel's *Valses Nobles et Sentimentales* (example 97). Here the pattern of downbeat accelerando and upbeat luftpause enhances the dynamic intensity of the music and the thrust of the initial rhythmic figures.

[4] According to Carl Czerny, the famous piano pedagogue and student of Beethoven, the composer himself played this passage in a similar manner. See Carl Czerny, *On the Proper Performance of All Beethoven Works for the Piano* (Paul Badura-Skoda, ed., Vienna: Wiener Urtext Ausgabe, 1970), pp. 104–105.

EX. 97 Ravel, *Valses Nobles et Sentimentales,* No. I (*Copyright 1912 Durand S.A. Used by permission of the agent, Theodore Presser Company.*)

Grace Notes

The examples illustrated thus far involve relatively *subtle* distinctions that call for relatively *slight* adjustments in the metric positions of tones. In each case the rhythmic patterns must retain their integrity within the musical structure. They should not be confused, therefore, with grace note embellishments, which have only an ornamental function.

These differences are evident in the theme from Beethoven's funeral march, illustrated in example 98A. The bass line of the theme begins with a series of triplet *grace note* figures (measures 1–3). These are changed into a pattern of stronger 32nd-note *anticipations* (measures 3 and 4), and these are followed by an even stronger 32nd-note *upbeat* figure (measure 5), thus creating a sequence of functions that progressively reinforces the developing musical momentum.)

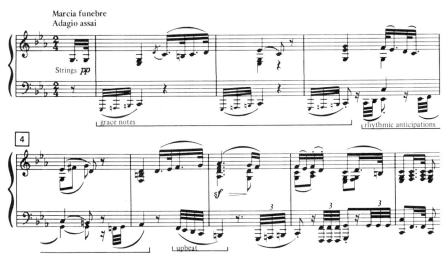

EX. 98A Beethoven, *Symphony No. 3,* 2nd mvt.

The function of these impulses should be made clear in performance by their placement in relation to the tones of resolution that follow. For example, the initial grace note figures should be entirely focused upon and absorbed into the following downbeat release. The 32nd-note anticipations, however, should retain their rhythmic independence in spite of the fact that they, too, must be placed close to their focal point of impact. The 32nd-note upbeat figure in measure 5, on the other hand, must retain its rhythmic *and* metric independence. These tones should be stretched to their full value so as to prepare for the climactic sforzando release on the downbeat of measure 6 (example 98B).

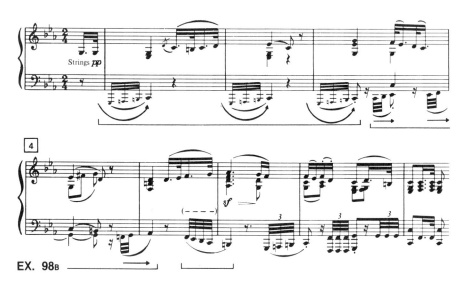

EX. 98B

The 32nd-note triplet figures beginning at the end of measure 6 should also maintain their notated metric position, but for a different reason. These rhythmic figures prepare the way for a similar accompaniment pattern in the second statement of the theme, a pattern that represents the regular, inexorable cadence of the funeral drums (example 98C).

EX. 98c   (second statement)

Tempo

Tempo has a great deal to do with the way in which these rhythmic patterns are performed. Example 99, for instance, might be played at a rather slow tempo, with four beats to the measure, or at a somewhat faster tempo, with two beats to the measure. In the first instance the final eighth note in measure 2 would be performed as an upbeat figure, with perhaps a slight luftpause just before the downbeat release. In the second instance the same eighth note would be played as a rhythmic anticipation, and placed closer to the following downbeat release.

In 4 . . .

EX. 99A   Mendelssohn, *Ruy Blas* Overture

In 2 . . .

EX. 99B

The effect of tempo can also be seen in example 100. In this case, because of the fast pace of the music, the last eighth note in each bar is clearly established as a quick, thrusting rhythmic anticipation. However, the sudden ritard in measure 59 alters the function and significance of this eighth note. Here it should be played as a strong metric upbeat, and separated quite markedly from the following downbeat release to enhance the arrival of this important climactic focal point. This effect can be achieved only if the return to tempo does not begin until the downbeat of measure 60; otherwise the entire effect is lost.

115

EX. 100 Ravel, *Valses Nobles et Sentimentales,* No. VII (*Copyright 1912 Durand S.A. Used by permission of the agent, Theodore Presser Company.*)

HIGHER-LEVEL RELATIONSHIPS

Rubato is often used to reinforce the momentum of repetitive patterns. Example 101, for instance, is based upon a rising chromatic line that is repeated three times with slight alterations of harmony, accentuation, and instrumentation. Here a subtle ritard at the end of the first phrase and a more obvious one before each successive release support the cumulative thrust of the progression and reinforce the final climactic resolution.

The momentum of repetitive melodies can also be enhanced at the beginning of the sequence. This is true of the Tchaikowsky melody in example 102. A slow beginning of this theme along with a gradual acceleration reinforces the forward momentum of the music.

A similar pattern may be used in the Tchaikowsky theme of example 103. The first phrase of this melody might be performed with a tenuto at the beginning of its action and an accelerando toward the first forte release.

116

EX. 101 Beethoven, *Symphony No. 3,* 1st mvt.

EX. 102 Tchaikowsky, *Symphony No. 5,* 3rd mvt.

The second phrase should contain a stronger crescendo, and might include a rubato ritard at the end of its motion in support of the final suppressed resolution. This shaping helps to join the two phrases into a single eight-measure pattern.

Similar adjustments should be made in all higher-level patterns. Indeed, rubato shadings must always be geared to the level of development as well as to the quality of motion. One of the most obvious uses of the ritard, for example, occurs at the end of a composition. And although it is often overdone, the use of a ritard at this point helps to insure the complete release of all accumulated tension. However, these rallentandos must be played in proportion to the dynamic development and character of the entire movement or piece.

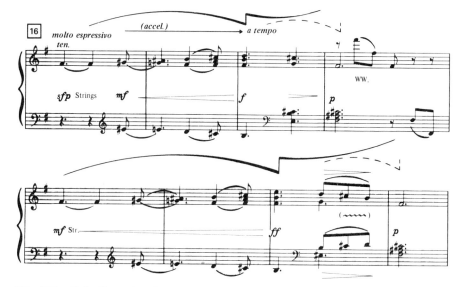

EX. 103 Tchaikowsky, *Symphony No. 5,* 1st mvt.

Unfortunately, strong rallentandos are often used even when the principal release occurs at an earlier point within the progression. This often happens at the ends of concerto movements, and in other pieces where a repeated cadential pattern is sufficient to fully resolve all accumulated tensions. In the Beethoven *Choral Fantasy* of example 104, for instance, the last tonal impulse is enhanced by an increase in the rhythmic pace of the music, so that a final ritard seems particularly inappropriate here.

EX. 104 Beethoven, *Choral Fantasy*

The same principle may be illustrated by comparing different performances of the Tchaikowsky excerpt in example 105. Because of the
dramatic character of the music, a strong ritard at the end of this movement is certainly appropriate.) But of the two versions that are normally
used, the first is more effective because its thrust is centered upon the first
tonic release, which occurs on a strong hypermetric pulse (example 105A).

EX. 105A   Tchaikowsky, *Nutcracker,* "Valse des Fleurs"

In the second version, the primary thrust is focused upon a repetition
of the tonic chord that falls upon a weak hypermetric pulse, and is therefore
less effective (example 105B).)

EX. 105B

STYLISTIC CONSIDERATIONS

Like all expressive techniques, rubato must be geared to the style of the
music and the character of the composition. Many Baroque pieces, for example, would be distorted by gross variations in tempo.) However, subtle
rubato adjustments are appropriate here as they are in all styles of music.
According to Joachim Quantz, a famous flutist and theoretician of the
period, "The performance should be easy and flexible . . . without stiffness
and constraint."

In 1615 Frescobaldi wrote:

This kind of playing must not be subject to the beat [but taken] now slowly, now quickly, and even held in the air, to match the expressive effects . . .

In 1753, C.P.E. Bach wrote:

Certain deliberate disturbances of the beat are extremely beautiful . . .
    Certain notes and rests should be prolonged beyond their written length for reasons of expression.
    [Certain sequential passages] can be effectively performed by accelerating gradually and gently, and retarding immediately afterwards.
    [However, he warns us:]
    . . . in spite of beautiful details [of flexible tempo] to hold the tempo at the end of a piece just as it was at the start, which is a very difficult achievement.

Special care must be taken in Baroque music to articulate the internal subdivisions of the phrase; however, this must be done without disturbing the rhythmic momentum of the music.) In sequential passages this can be accomplished by inserting slight pauses between the motivic patterns, or, more subtly, by delicately shading the final tones of each impulse (example 106).

EX. 106   Bach, *Invention No. 1 in C Major*

It must be kept in mind that the lack of expression marks in these scores does not indicate a lack of expressivity) According to contemporary accounts, expressive nuances were expected to be added by the performer (just as they are today in the performance of a play or drama).) The manner in which this was accomplished played an important role in how the performer's musical abilities were judged.)
    Quantz:

Good execution must be *diversified*. Light and shadow must be continuously interchanged. For in truth you will never move the listener if you render all the notes at the same strength or the same weakness; if you perform, so to speak, always in the same colour, or do not know how to raise or moderate the tone at the proper time.)

C.P.E. Bach:

> Keyboardists whose chief asset is mere technique are clearly at a disadvantage. A performer may have the most agile fingers, be competent at single and double trills, master the art of fingering, read skillfully at sight regardless of the key, and transpose extemporaneously without the slightest difficulty; and yet he may be something less than a clear, pleasing, or stirring keyboardist. More often than not, one meets technicians, nimble keyboardists by profession, who possess all of these qualifications and indeed astound us with their prowess without ever touching our sensibilities. They overwhelm our hearing without satisfying it and stun the mind without moving it. A mere technician can lay no claim to the rewards of those who sway in gentle undulation the ear rather than the eye, the heart rather than the ear, and lead it where they will.[5]

Classical music, too, is enhanced by judiciously applied expressive inflections.

Leopold Mozart:

> Every care must be taken to find and to render the affect which the composer wished to have brought out . . . Indeed, one must know how to change from soft to loud without directions and of one's own accord, each at the right time; for this, in the familiar language of painters, means *light* and *shade.*

Wolfgang Mozart:

> Would you like to know how I have expressed and even indicated the beating, loving heart? By two violins playing in octaves . . . You feel the trembling—the faltering—you see how the throbbing breast begins to heave; this I have indicated by a crescendo. You hear the whispering and the sighing.
> [However] . . . passions, whether violent or not, must never be expressed in such a way as to invite disgust, [so] music, even in the most terrible situations, must never offend the ear, but must please the hearer, or in other words must never cease to be music.[6]

Romantic and Expressionistic works often require strong dramatic reinforcement. Yet here, too, it is essential to balance the tensive character of the music against the ongoing momentum of the piece, so that both the expressive tone *and* the dynamic thrust of the work are enhanced. These internal shapings should be strong enough to reinforce the dramatic character of the music, but they must never be exaggerated to the point where they detract from its ongoing development.

[5] From C.P.E. Bach, *Essay on the True Art of Playing Keyboard Instruments,* ed., trans. William J. Mitchell (New York: W. W. Norton & Co. Inc., 1948), from the chapter entitled "Performance."

[6] For further discussion see chapter one on expression and chapter eleven on performance in Leonard G. Ratner's *Classic Music: Expression, Form, and Style* (New York: G. Schirmer Inc., 1980).

If the internal impulses are reinforced at the expense of higher-level actions, the performance may seem immature or superficial. The performer may seem so concerned with incidental goals that he misses the significance of the overall endeavor. With excessive or imbalanced rubato, a performance sounds ludicrous. The actions don't feel natural, they don't seem to result from the musical impulse, they seem exaggerated in relation to the goals. The music may sound insincere and sentimental, like the performance of an actor who is overacting, or who doesn't understand the motives of the character he is portraying.

On the other hand, if these interior shapes are ignored, the momentum of the piece may never really develop. The performance may never seem to get off the ground. Because our attention and interest is not coaxed and guided on the lower levels of the piece, the higher-level resolutions seem disappointing. There may not be enough tension to sustain a forceful release. With no rubato, the musical actions sound stilted. Instead of striving, purposeful motions, the music seems lifeless and mechanical, like the movements of a ''wind-up'' toy doll that has been designed to imitate the outward motions of people, but which cannot reflect the self-generated, motivated quality of those actions.

The effective use of rubato results in a musical performance, a *human* performance, one that is neither mechanical nor sentimental, one that captures the real feeling of the piece and reflects the true nature of significant human emotions. A keen sense of rubato is one of the most sensitive aspects of performance and one of the most crucial elements of the entire musical experience.

CHAPTER 6

The Dynamic Impulse

During the course of this book we have been concerned with those factors that affect the expressive character and dynamic form of musical progressions. We have seen how factors such as melodic contour, harmony, meter, rhythm, and style affect the shaping of phrases and how elements such as volume and rubato can be used to reinforce the evolution of a developing musical sequence. We have seen these elements used in a variety of contexts, in excerpts taken from a number of different styles and periods.

However, if the performer is to arrive at a truly effective interpretation, he must look at the structure of complete compositions.) The performer must continually ask himself how the compositional elements combine to form a single musical entity, and he must try to determine the function of each internal pattern in relation to the entire piece.)

REINFORCING THE MUSICAL FORM

If he is to reinforce the dynamic form of a composition, the performer must learn to gauge the significance of each musical impulse at every stage of its musical development. For instance, the opening measures of Beethoven's *String Quartet in F Major* (example 107A), might be phrased in either of two ways.

Either this . . .

EX. 107A   Beethoven, *String Quartet in F Major,* Op. 18 No.1, 1st mvt.

124

or this . . .

EX. 107A (continued)

In past chapters we have seen that the phrasing of a motive such as this depends largely upon its *position within the composition.* In the beginning of this piece, for example, the motive is best shaped in a way that creates a suppressed dynamic tendency that can be reinforced later in the piece (example 107B).[1]

EX. 107B

In the exposition of this movement these tendencies are exploited in a variety of ways. To enhance the evolutionary process, the forward thrusts of the motive in measures 5–8 and 13–16 should be gently reinforced, and the subito piano in bar 20 and the sforzando overemphases in bars 22–27 should appear as sudden, unexpected interjections. The forward thrust of the last three bars should be reinforced, but to no more than a forte, for this is only the first climactic release in the movement (example 107C).

EX. 107C

[1] On the other hand the general character of the music (''Allegro con brio'') calls for a consistent reinforcement of its lower-level patterns. That is to say, the suppression of this impulse should not be overdone.

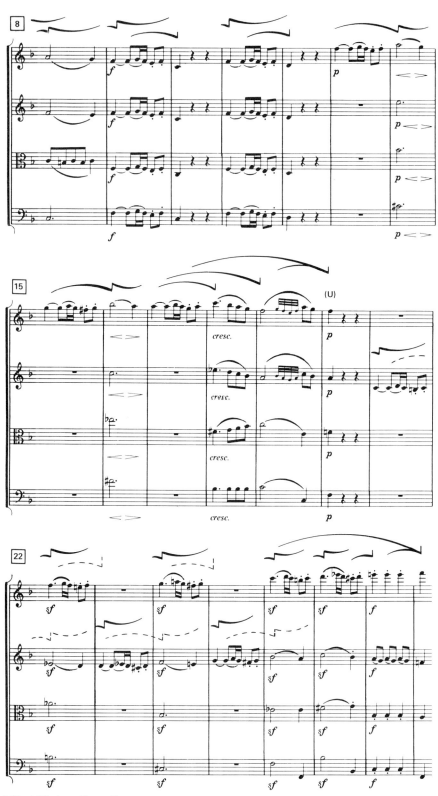

EX. 107c (continued)

The forward momentum of the motive is further exploited in the development section. Here the ongoing thrust of the music should be continually underscored to maintain that sense of driving momentum that is an essential characteristic of developmental and transitional passages (example 107D).

EX. 107D

EX. 107D (continued)

The recapitulation contains the first fortissimo statement of the composition. Here the forward thrust of the motive should be reinforced so as to underscore the fulfillment of its initial dynamic implications (example 107E).

However, this fulfillment is short-lived, for the music immediately reverts to its gentle, teasing melodic curves and suppressed resolutions (example 107F).

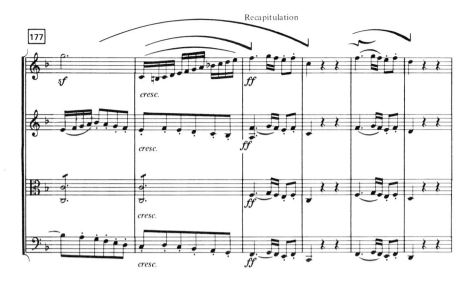

EX. 107ᴇ

EX. 107ꜰ

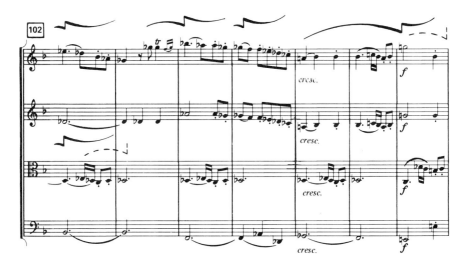

EX. 107F (continued)

The full resolution of the principal motive must await the coda of the movement. Here the forward thrust of the theme is enhanced through a series of melodic and intervallic expansions, a group of sforzando accentuations, and a final stretto sequence that ends with three weak-beat syncopations. These final thrusts should be clearly underscored so as to provide a satisfying conclusion to the dynamic form of the movement (example 107G).

EX. 107G

EX. 107G (continued)

The suppressed dynamic tendencies of the theme from Beethoven's *Symphony No. 8* (example 108A), play a similar role in the development of the composition. (This theme was originally analyzed in example 19.)

EX. 108A Beethoven, *Symphony No. 8,* 1st mvt.

The suppressed impulses of this progression are also an integral part of the second theme of the movement (example 108B).

EX. 108ʙ

These inhibited thrusts are extensively exploited in the development section. Here again the constant forward momentum of the music must be maintained (example 108C).

EX. 108ᴄ

EX. 108c (continued)

Again, the dynamic tendencies are forcefully resolved at the beginning of the recapitulation. But this resolution does not last long, for the rising impulse is soon exploited with the appearance of the subito forte in measure 201 and the subito piano in measure 202 (example 108D).

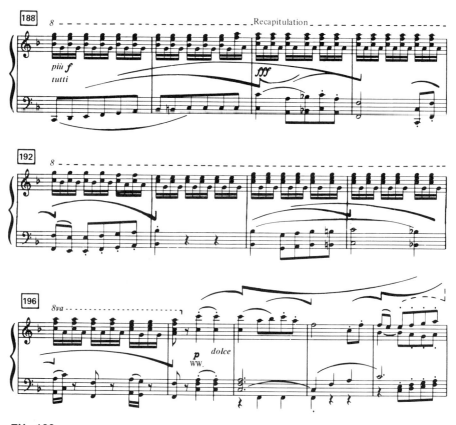

EX. 108d

EX. 108ᴅ (continued)

After further expansion and development this motive is finally gently resolved in the last cadential sequence (example 108E).

EX. 108ᴇ

EX. 108E (continued)

Sometimes the suppressed dynamic implications of a musical impulse may have to wait for several movements before they are completely fulfilled. The suppressed tendencies in the introductory theme of Tchaikowsky's *Symphony No. 5,* for example, must await the end of the last movement for their final resolution. The suppressed impulse in this instance is created by the downward scale pattern in the second half of the introductory theme. The forward thrust of this scale is suppressed by the decrescendo in bar 5 and again in bar 7 (example 109A).

EX. 109A   Tchaikowsky, *Symphony No. 5,* 1st mvt.

This pattern is repeated several times, but its dynamic implications are not fulfilled; in fact they are only aggravated by the sudden sforzando overemphases in measures 28 and 30 (example 109B).

EX. 109B

This theme occurs in various places throughout the symphony, but its forward thrust is not fully realized until the final triumphant march at the end of the last movement (example 109C).

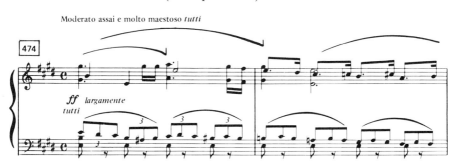

EX. 109c   4th mvt.

EX. 109c (continued)

Alternative Patterns of Evolution

Of course, compositions don't *always* start with suppressed introductory impulses. Beethoven's Fifth Symphony, for example, begins with a forceful end-accented motive that should be strongly reinforced from its very first appearance. Tension is created here by the accumulating thrust of the motive beginning in measure 6, and by the fact that *no crescendo* is called for in these measures. Here the gathering force of the music must be held in check until the sudden crescendo-forte in bars 18–19 (example 110A).

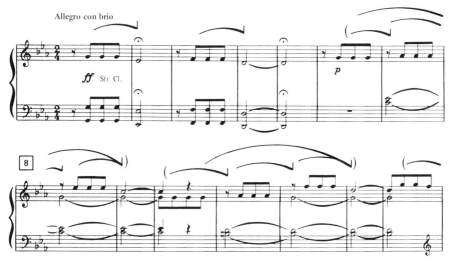

EX. 110A   Beethoven, *Symphony No. 5,* 1st mvt.

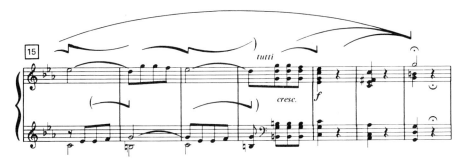

EX. 110A (continued)

The performer must take special care to avoid a premature crescendo here and in similar sections elsewhere in the movement, for these suppressed crescendos and sudden forte releases are essential to the dynamic form of the piece. They reappear at the end of the development section (example 110B) and again at the very end of the coda, where they set the stage for the final cadential sequence (example 110C).

EX. 110B

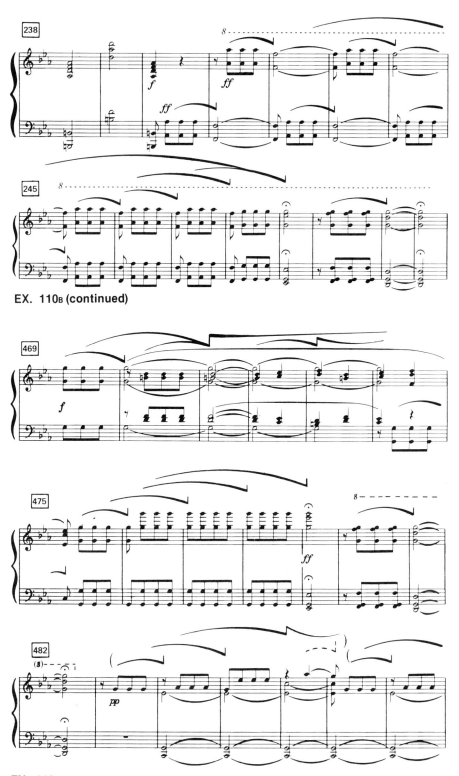

EX. 110B (continued)

EX. 110C

EX. 110c (continued)

The following excerpt from Franck's *D Minor Symphony* (example 111A) is also based upon a motive that should be played as an end-accented impulse from the beginning of the piece. Here the slow tempo favors the development of an end-accented motive, and, also, the melody must gather enough momentum to extend into the primary release on the downbeat of measure 4.

'Cellos and Basses

EX. 111A Franck, *Symphony in D Minor,* 1st mvt.

The nature of this motive changes radically during the course of the movement. In fact, the exposition of the primary theme contains a reversal of its basic shape and character. Because of the allegro tempo and the emphatic quality of the music, the motive is now beginning-accented; yet it leads to a forceful end-accented impulse, reinforced here by the double-dotted sequence at the end of the progression (example 111B).

EX. 111B .

EX. 111ʙ (continued)

After an extensive development, the ambivalent nature of this motive is finally resolved at the end of the movement in a series of imitative, end-accented thrusts (example 111C).

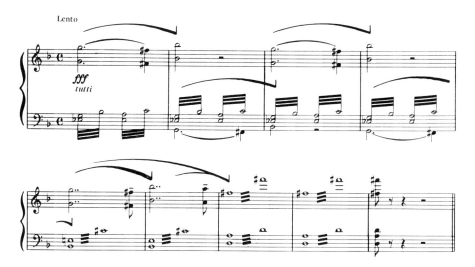

EX. 111c

REPEATED THEMATIC STATEMENTS

The relationship between restatements of a theme is always an important factor in the development of a musical structure. Often these restatements include a simple reshaping of the melody according to its position within the piece. In example 112A, from Dvořák's *New World Symphony,* the composer shapes the theme so that it contains a suppressed dynamic tendency that is focused on the third downbeat of the phrase.

When this theme reappears in the recapitulation, it is shaped in a way that reinforces this suppressed tendency (example 112B).

EX. 112A Dvořák, *New World Symphony*, 4th mvt. (exposition)

EX. 112B (recapitulation)

The same is true of the following Tchaikowsky themes. In the exposition of the melody in example 113A, the diminuendo in measure 94 prevents a full resolution of the suppressed tendencies of the early measures.

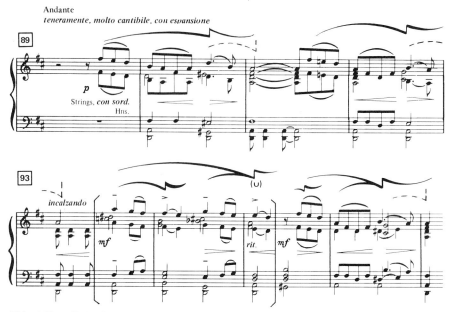

EX. 113A Tchaikowsky, *Symphony No. 6,* 1st mvt. (exposition)

This thrust is resolved in the recapitulated version of the theme (example 113B).

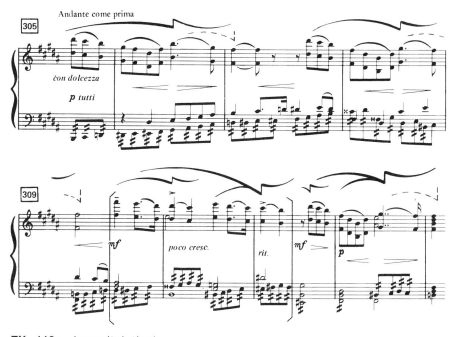

EX. 113B (recapitulation)

In example 114A the diminuendo in measure 19 prevents the final resolution of the suppressed tendencies in the exposition of the theme.

EX. 114A   Tchaikowsky, *Symphony No. 4,* 2nd mvt.

However, there is *no* diminuendo in the final thematic statement (example 114B). Players who ignore the diminuendos in the expositions of these two themes disregard an important aspect of the dynamic evolution of these compositions.[2]

EX. 114B

[2] The same principle applies to *exact* repetitions of themes. That is to say, even exact restatements should never be played the same way twice, for each statement has a different musical function according to its position within the composition. The performer must determine the function of each statement in relation to the dynamic form of the entire piece.

EX. 114ʙ (continued)

Incipient Thematic Relationships

As we have seen, important dynamic relationships often exist between the different themes of a work. These may involve a simple restatement of the dynamic patterns of a motive, as in Beethoven's *Symphony No. 8* (example 108), or they may involve a more complex dynamic relationship. In the next example the relationship of the themes plays an important role in the dynamic evolution of the entire movement, and indeed, of the entire symphony. The opening melody of this movement might be shaped with the principal accent on the fourth downbeat of the phrase (example 115A).

EX. 115ᴀ   Beethoven, *Symphony No. 5,* 3rd mvt.

But it is more effective when performed as indicated in example 115B, since this version contains a suppressed thrust that can be exploited later on.

EX. 115ʙ

This potential is immediately reinforced with the appearance of the second theme, which also happens to be the motto of the entire symphony (example 115C).

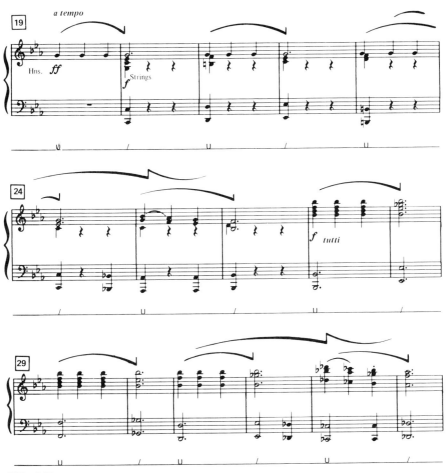

EX. 115ᴄ

The relationship between these two melodies is the key factor in the dynamic form of the movement. This is made clear when both themes reappear together in measure 101.) Here the motto theme, now serving as an accompaniment melody, is forced to assume a rather unnatural, beginning-accented shape (example 115D).

EX. 115D

However, the forward momentum of the motive soon emerges in an expanding sequence, enabling the section to end with a series of reiterated end-accented thrusts (example 115E).

EX. 115E

EX. 115E (continued)

After a trio section that further exploits the forward thrust of this impulse,[3] the melodies return in the recapitulation of the movement. Here it is better to shape the motto theme as a beginning-accented phrase because of its shortened final tone and the addition of an accompaniment pattern in the initial measure. (Compare the beginning of example 115F with the expository statement at the beginning of example 115C. Notice the different hypermetric position of the motive.)

[3] See example 52.

EX. 115F

Once again the forward thrust of this motive rises to the surface, but this time there is an important difference; now the music begins *sempre pp* in preparation for the transition to the final movement of the symphony. As a result, the scherzo movement in general, and this final section in particular, serve as a long anacrusis to the forceful, affirmative, end-accented finale (example 115G).

EX. 115G

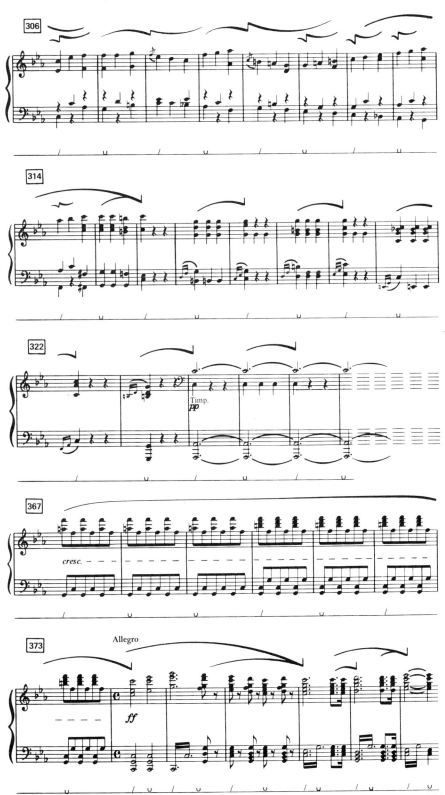

EX. 115G (continued)

A similar relationship exists between the themes of Brahms' *Symphony No. 3*, fourth movement. In this case a potential dynamic thrust is contained in the first chromatic rise of the "sotto voce" theme, here centered on the second beat of the measure (example 116A).

EX. 116A Brahms, *Symphony No. 3*, 4th mvt.

This potential thrust is underscored in the next appearance of the theme (example 116B). Here the focal point is enhanced by expanding its duration (bar 9) and by shifting it to the downbeat of the phrase (bar 13).

EX. 116B

The chromatic motive is the germinating force of the transitional theme of the exposition. Here the melody is located in the alto and tenor voices of the texture (example 116C).

EX. 116c

The same motive is the basis of the subordinate theme as well, although here its chromatic thrust has been expanded to form an arpeggiated noncongruent pattern (example 116D).

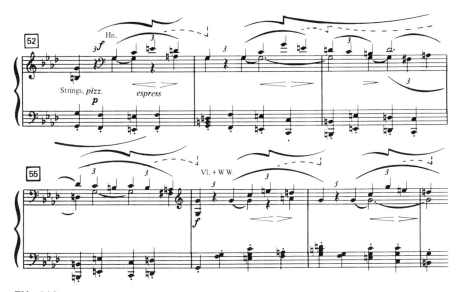

EX. 116d

This impulse also serves as the basis of the development section. The principal sequence begins with a completely suppressed, beginning-accented version of the motive (example 116E) and gradually evolves, through a series of ascending and descending patterns, to climax in the recapitulation of the movement (example 116F).

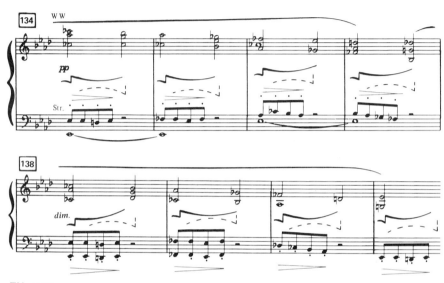

EX. 116E

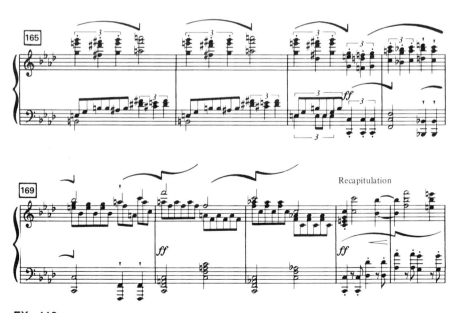

EX. 116F

EX. 116ꜰ (continued)

The motive reappears in the coda in both its duplet and triplet forms. Now, however, its structure is expanded intermittently to become fully congruent with the metric structure and to gently fulfill its inherent dynamic potential (example 116G).

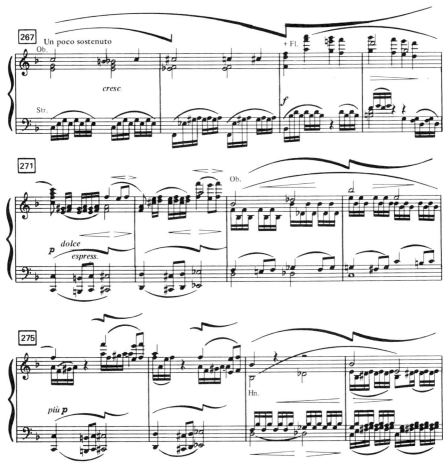

EX. 116ɢ

EX. 116ɢ (continued)

EX. 116G (continued)

The important point in each of these analyses is not simply the shape of a particular phrase. Rather, the question is one of how a particular theme contributes to the development of the ongoing musical line. In each case the performer must try to determine the dynamic form of the entire musical structure and then consistently reinforce those aspects of the piece that will enhance its overall evolution. He must gauge the function of each internal pattern and the significance of each resolution, and blend them all into a single, organic, cohesive musical statement.

CHAPTER 7

Performance Techniques

Technique that is divorced from musical expression is of little value. Technique is never a goal itself, but always a means to a specific musical end.

Creating an expressive performance is the process of a performer giving a vibrant, living presence to the music. It is based upon the performer's ability to create a series of goal-oriented actions that develop within a single, unified, organic musical impulse.

Every accomplished performer spends a great deal of time and effort mastering the technical aspects of his art. Each understands the importance of good technical facility and none would deny the value of attaining a flawless technique. Yet every serious artist also realizes that a technique which is divorced from musical expression is of little value. To these performers, technique is never a goal in itself, but always a means to a specific musical end.

The specific techniques used to create an expressive performance vary, of course, from instrument to instrument; however, the basic principles of musical expression remain the same. This process, we have seen, depends upon the ability of the performer to create a vibrant, living presence within the music. It is based upon his ability to create a series of goal-oriented actions that develop within a single, unified, organic musical impulse.

The performer must never let the physical limitations of his instrument dictate the expressive form of the music. The pianist must overcome the percussive nature of his instrument so as to develop a lyrical musical line. The string player must not let the length of his bow determine the shape of his phrases. Brass and woodwind players must overcome problems of breath, embouchure, and attack in an effort to create the most expressive tonal patterns. Singers must avoid all mannerisms that interrupt the natural flow of the musical action or contradict the expressive implications of the tonal impulse. The performer must use the technical capabilities of his instrument to enhance the character of the piece as determined by the tonal relationships that exist within its musical structure. Some specific suggestions for the major performance media are outlined in the following sections of this chapter.

THE PRINCIPAL PERFORMANCE MEDIA

Piano

The subject of piano technique has been controversial almost from the beginning of its development. Virtually all of the early masters of the piano had definite ideas about the posture of the body, the position of the arms and hands, the functioning of the fingers, and the kinds of motions that produce the most effective results. Many of these early pianists felt, for example, that one should play with curved fingers, striking the key with the ends of the fingertips. Others (Chopin among them) favored a flat finger position in which the key is struck with the fleshy "pad" of the finger. Almost all of those artists felt that the manner in which the key was depressed determined the kind of sound produced.

Most contemporary pianists also feel that their touch directly affects the quality of the resulting piano tone. There is no physical evidence to support this view. However there is no doubt that the way tones are *combined* does directly affect the quality of the sounds produced.

In the case of finger and hand position, for example, it is generally better to use a flat finger position in pianissimo and legato passages, for this position provides more resilience and helps keep the finger in continuous contact with the key, allowing a maximum amount of control over the striking mechanism. A curved finger position, on the other hand, facilitates changing the hand position in rapid sequences and provides more power in fortissimo passages.

The various effects achieved from tone combinations depend upon a variety of physical and psychological factors. For example, the illusion of a more brilliant sound can be achieved by reinforcing the highest note of a chord. Higher tones tend to reverberate for a shorter period of time and may seem slighted if played at equal intensity with the other notes. The same is true of a melody that appears over an accompaniment. (Lower tones, you will remember, carry more weight than higher tones.) The quality of dissonant chords can be enhanced if the tones of the dissonant interval are subtly reinforced.

Other illusions can be created by drawing attention to different aspects of the musical structure. Slight variations in timing and dynamics can call attention to a principal melodic pattern or a particularly significant rhythmic impulse without distorting the basic tonal relationships of the piece. These subtle shifts in the placement and reinforcement of tones are a principal element in the development of an expressive piano technique.

Perhaps the greatest illusion of all is the impression of a continuous legato line. The piano, after all, is a percussive instrument. A very strong impression of legato can be obtained, however, if each tone of a series is carefully blended in terms of length and dynamics with all other tones in

Being Centered

the series.) Phrase shaping plays an important role in this process, for it must be remembered that listeners hear selectively, in a directional, goal-oriented manner. If these projections and expectations are carefully enhanced and exploited, a very strong sense of musical flow and continuity can be created.

Imagery can be an important aid in achieving this effect. Pianists should sing the melody inwardly or, as Beethoven suggested, imagine the tonal coloring achieved by a violinist or wind player.) The performer should breathe with each phrase, and consistently strive to extend the musical line into the principal focal points of the piece. The pianist must take special care to taper the ends of phrases so as to make clear the internal structure of the music.

In legato playing, the keys should be gently depressed rather than struck and the fingers should remain in close contact with the keys.) The entire line should be played in a single curve or sweep of motion, with the wrist rotating in a smooth, flexible manner. All motion should be kept to a minimum and the action coordinated in one continuous impulse.

Use of the damper pedal can reinforce the illusion of legato, but this pedal must never be allowed to blur the fundamental rhythm.) Indeed, the damper pedal, and the soft pedal as well, should be used as much to alter the tone quality of the piano as to enhance the technical abilities of the pianist.

In playing staccato passages, the hand must be firm and the wrist flexible. The fingers should be kept close to the keys to avoid noisy, unmusical effects.) In other contexts, extraneous noise can be minimized by holding (but not *pressing*) the key down for the full duration of the note. Indeed, pianists should become as concerned with the release of tones as they are with their inception.

In terms of intensity of motion, attention should shift to different parts of the body according to the kind of passage being played. The fingers can move with the greatest agility, and should be the principal source of activity in fast, rapidly changing patterns.) However, the fingers should never reach for the keys; phrase patterns should always be prepared by the motion of the lower arm and hand.) The upper arm and shoulder can provide more power than the extremities, and should be the primary source of intensity in louder, slower passages.) Energy should flow easily through the system to focus directly onto the point of tonal attack.

Whatever the focal point of motion, all of the performer's movements should emanate from deep within his body, so that his actions become an extension of his innermost muscular impulses.[1] At the same time, there

---

[1] This "center-to-periphery" concept is based upon the nature of the musical experience. Listening to music, we have seen, is based upon a series of interlocking tensive reactions, expectations, and projections which occur in the mind and body of the listener. If the music is generated through similar tensive impulses, a very direct kind of communication is set up between the performer and his audience.

should be an economy of motion in the extremities. As little effort as possible should be expended, and each motion should be used to maximum effect. The body must be kept relaxed in the sense that there be no unwarranted tightness or stiffness, for such tension fatigues the body and inhibits the flow of energy. The pianist should allow his muscles to expand and contract with the musical flow so that tension is kept at a minimum during the pauses that occur within the musical sequence.

Ultimately, the performer should lose consciousness of all technical details and become fully absorbed in the evolution of the composition. He should always try to feel the piece in terms of a single, fundamental musical impulse. Despite his careful attention to internal phrases, he must constantly keep in mind the shape of the entire work so that he can present a unified, cohesive musical statement.

Strings

The single most important factor in expressive string performance is the ability of the performer to obtain the maximum amount of intensity and resonance with the bow, with a minimum amount of expended physical energy. This principle of economy of means is important in every performance medium, but it is particularly important in string playing, for here the phrasing and articulation of the music depend directly upon getting the maximum amount of tonal energy out of each bow stroke. The player must have total control of his bowing action, for this motion is his principal means of reinforcing the character and shape of the musical impulse.

One of the most common errors encountered in string performance is the tendency of players to make an automatic crescendo and decrescendo with each bow stroke (example 117). This effect is especially noticeable at the end of the stroke. On the downbow, too much bow is often used at the beginning of the stroke, so that the last notes of the stroke are much weaker than the earlier ones. To correct this habit, the player should maintain a more even speed throughout the bow. He should also overcompensate somewhat, giving the first half of the motion slightly less bow than the second half while increasing bow pressure to maintain the same intensity.

EX. 117

A related problem is the use of a crescendo with all upbows. Here, the swell can be smoothed out by moving the bow a little faster and with more pressure at the top third, and easing off a little toward the middle, where the bow is more lively. When used correctly, these natural features of the

Bowing: Speed, Weight, + Placement

bowing action can be an effective aid to phrasing; but the player should take care to avoid these effects when they contradict the natural implications of the musical line.

In legato passages, the player must avoid pauses or accents between bow strokes. In particular, he must not shorten the last tone of an upbow anacrusis in preparation for the change to the following downbow release. Instead, he must extend the sound to the very end of the anacrusis and delay the bow change until the last possible moment.

Bowing problems often arise because of the unequal length of bow strokes. In example 118, the length of the downbow is three times that of the upbow. As a result, the quarter notes tend to receive too much emphasis. This problem can be overcome by using less weight on the upbow strokes and by placing the bow slightly farther from the bridge. The player must develop the ability to vary the length of the bow stroke without varying the dynamic level of the sound.

EX. 118

Players should not feel obligated to use the entire bow for each bow stroke. In initial phrases that begin with short anacruses, they should start the phrase near the middle of the bow and should not hesitate to reposition the bow during pauses within the musical line whenever this will result in more effective phrase patterns.

The player should use the various sections of the bow to enhance the character of the music—the tip for lightness and grace and the lower portion for heavier, more forceful passages. He should avoid frequent bow changes that interfere with the "long line" of the music. During long legato passages, orchestral players might "stagger" their bow changes to maintain the tonal continuity.

The string player should always try to gear the quality of his bowing to the style of the composition. He should adjust the bow strokes in terms of speed, weight, and placement according to the character of the music. Fast, light bow strokes near the fingerboard, for example, give a light, airy sound. A heavier, slower stroke closer to the bridge creates a dense, heavy quality. These three factors (speed, weight, and placement) should be varied continually according to the nature of the musical action.[2]

Vibrato should also be geared to the character of the music. A slower, wider vibrato is often effective in broad legato passages, while a faster, narrow vibrato provides a more brilliant, energetic tone. The player should

---

[2] Specific types of articulation are discussed later in this chapter under the heading marked "Conducting."

continually alter the speed and amplitude of the vibrato to match the expressive implications of the music. The vibrato should not be used continuously. Its purpose is to add vibrancy and vitality to the sound, and its constant, unvaried use soon becomes boring.)

String players, and other performers as well, must remember to use *all* of the musical elements to reinforce the shape and character of the music. Certain "secondary" forms of accentuation such as tone and resonance emphases, durational accents, vibrato stresses, finger accents, and similar nuances are indispensable expressive techniques and should be used along with other, more obvious changes of pace and dynamics.

It is particularly important in string playing to remember that all technical effects are simply the means to an expressive musical end. The player must never lose sight of his ultimate goal. He must constantly listen to his playing, and try to match his performance to his mental image of the piece. He must train his ear to be as objective as possible in comparing the actual performance to his mental conception of the music.

Winds

A key element in performing effectively on wind instruments is good breath control. This process is based upon the proper use of the diaphragm and related abdominal muscles. In wind playing, proper diaphragmatic breathing provides a reservoir of air that can support a strong, consistent, resonant sound. At the same time, this kind of support frees the embouchure for the more subtle aspects of phrasing and articulation that are essential to an expressive performance.)

Proper breath control begins with a firm diaphragmatic base. The performer should begin inhalation with an outward and downward expansion of the abdomen, and avoid raising or "hunching up" the shoulders. (Students might be told to breathe "low in the mouth." This has no anatomical significance, but it helps to create the right conditions for proper inhalation.) The mouth, throat, and tongue should remain flexible and tension–free so that they can control the speed and direction of the breath.

Inadequate breath control can lead to poor phrasing as well as poor tone quality and poor intonation. The last tones of a phrase, for example, may be too short, weak, or out of tune because the player does not have enough remaining breath, or sufficient *control* of his remaining breath, to support these notes properly. Brass players in particular should avoid the urge to expend all their breath at the beginning of the phrase. Instead, they should monitor their breath through the entire sequence, taking care to support the sound through the last tonal impulse.

The key to effective articulation resides in the relationship of diaphragm and embouchure. Rapid staccato passages, particularly when they are in the high register, are virtually impossible without firm diaphragmatic support) At the same time, the mouth and lips must remain firm but free of unwarranted tension.) The performer should employ the tongue sparingly, using only enough motion to insure the proper execution of the passage. With reed instruments, the lower jaw should not move in conjunction with the tongue.

Legato passages should be based upon a constant, uninterrupted flow of breath. The action of tongue and fingers should be lightly superimposed upon this continuous stream of air.) Indeed, in brass playing, more breath pressure should be supplied *between* the tones than on the tones themselves to offset the changing patterns of vibration that occur within the instrument.) This is riskier than starting each note with a new pulse of air pressure, but it is the only way to insure a continuous legato line. Horn players in particular should avoid a dynamic swell on each individual note. While it is true that long tones need direction, a swell on *every* note detracts from the ongoing musical line.[3]

Initial entrances, especially strong marcato attacks, must be adequately prepared *before* the onset of the sound. The performer must set the diaphragmatic muscles before the tone begins, then release the tension with a light, firm action of the tongue. Reed players should never let the tongue slap or hit the reed. For clean attacks, the performer should use only as much tongue movement as is necessary.)

Diaphragmatic support is crucial to playing effective pianissimo passages. The sounds should appear as a light, top layer that is gently riding upon a deep, strong undercurrent of support. The size of the embouchure is important here. In this case a very small opening, with a small amount of air flow, produces the softest sound. Reed players must take care to avoid the ''hard'' sound that comes from a tight, pinched embouchure.

In loud passages diaphragmatic support is less of a problem. The embouchure should be somewhat more flexible. The larynx should be open wide, allowing a larger volume of air to pass through, and lip pressure, especially in the brass, should be loose enough to allow for these larger vibrations. However, the player must not allow these changes in volume and pressure to alter the basic quality of sound. Performers must work to expand their dynamic range, but in performance they should never go beyond that point at which their tone quality begins to deteriorate.)

These variations in intensity also cause different intonational problems among the various instruments. Clarinets, for example, tend to become flat in fortissimo and sharp in pianissimo. Flutes tend to go sharp in fortissimo and flat in pianissimo. Performers must become aware of these general problems, as well as the specific idiosyncracies of their particular instruments, and make the necessary adjustments in embouchure, finger position, and breath control.

[3] This practice is similar to the ''messa di voce'' style of 17th century singers. The practice later became exaggerated to the point of affectation with violinists of the late Baroque Period.

Like other performers, wind players must learn to vary their tone quality according to the expressive character of the music. Wind performers too often maintain a single tonal coloration when in fact a change in quality to a rounder, warmer sound or a sharper, more brilliant sound would create a more appropriate expressive effect.[4] Here again, the performer must try to attain a good mental image of the desired effect and then gear his technique to produce this result. Good playing begins with the mind, extends through the technique, is judged by the ear, and reappears in terms of an adjusted technique.

Voice

Effective singing, like effective wind playing, is based largely upon the control and support of the entire breathing apparatus. Good breath support depends upon proper use and control of the diaphragmatic muscles and upon the unrestricted flow of air through an open, relaxed throat and mouth. Upon inhalation, the diaphragm is lowered and the abdomen expanded, filling the lower portion of the lungs with air. As more air is taken in, the upper chest, too, will expand; however, in no case should the chest or shoulders be raised or hunched up. This is the natural way to breathe, and nothing should be allowed to interfere with this process.

Air is expelled by contracting the abdomen and raising the diaphragm in a continuous, supportive motion. Since the throat tends to tighten with any physical effort, special care must be taken to keep the throat open and free of tension. The mouth cavity, too, should remain as large and open as possible. The tongue should lie flat and low in the mouth. The singer should have the sensation of directing the tone against the upper palate of the mouth, just behind the front teeth.

As a general rule, the singer should strive to maintain a constant, uninterrupted flow of breath, using the mouth and tongue to interject the syllables upon this continuous air stream. In marcato and staccato singing, *the throat must remain open,* the articulation created by a slight "bump" or pulse of the diaphragm. In melismatic passages, such as those illustrated in examples 119 and 120, an "h" inserted at the beginning of each note helps to establish the proper diaphragmatic action. However, once this technique is mastered, the "h's" should be dropped in favor of a continuous flow of sound.

One of the major faults in solo and choral performance is the lack of good enunciation. Singing has long been considered a natural extension of speech. In this context, singers must make every effort to ensure that the text is clearly understood.

---

[4] These qualities are directly affected by tongue position. A high position, as in the "ee" sound, produces a more brilliant sound. A low "aw" position creates a warmer quality.

EX. 119 Handel, *Messiah*, "Every Valley Shall Be Exalted"

EX. 120 Handel, *Messiah*, "For Unto Us a Child Is Born"

Good enunciation, first of all, requires correct pronunciation of the vowels. As a general rule, the pure vowel sound should be used. These sounds should not be distorted for the sake of ease of execution. Novice singers in particular will find that they will improve more rapidly if they use the pure vowel sounds throughout their range, and avoid changing the sound of the words to suit their particular vocal problems.

The consonants, on the other hand, call for a somewhat more specialized treatment. In choral singing particularly, some of the softer consonants must be reinforced if they are to be heard. For example, closed consonants such as *m, n, ng,* and *l* should be emphasized more strongly

167

than they are in normal speech; otherwise they may be lost.) When they appear at the end of words, these consonants should not be voiced (as in
a-men-*uh*), for this distorts the natural sound of the text.)

In words that begin with vowel sounds, the throat must remain open
at the beginning of the attack.) This can be assured by using a silent "h" at
the beginning of the word (as in [h]eleison).) This technique avoids a closed
throat or glottal attack, as well as the elision or slurring of words. However,
the singer should not use an audible "h," for this produces a breathy,
aspirated attack. For greater accuracy in soft attacks, the singer should try
to picture the sound in his head and prepare his body *before* the tone is produced.

When singing diphthongs, the singer should dwell on the first vowel
sound and move to the second vowel sound just before the release of the
note (as in high, *hah-ēē*). The same technique should be used when singing the final *r* (ever, *eh-vuh-r*). The nontonal, labial and dental consonants
such as *f, s,* and *z* should remain unaccented. These consonants do not produce a particularly pleasant or musical sound and should be as soft and
short as possible. On the other hand, the plosive consonants such as *d, t, p,*
and *b* should be clearly enunciated. When these consonants occur at the
end of words, it is usually best to place them just before or just after the beat
to avoid too strong an accent, as in example 121. The goal should always
be the clear, unaffected projection of the text.

Original notation:

EX. 121   Haydn, *The Creation*

Performed this way . . .

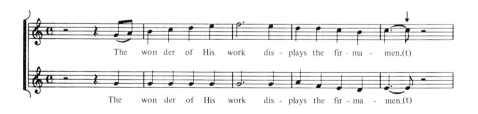

not this way . . .

EX. 121 (continued)

Another common fault of singers, both in solo and in ensemble performance, is the lack of clear, expressive phrasing. Too often the singer
seems so concerned with the production of the sound that he neglects this
vital aspect of performance. The singer must learn to phrase intelligently,
and to adjust his technique to the expressive demands of the score. Female
singers in particular must avoid an excessively wide vibrato, for such a
tremolo can obscure the musical line as well as the phrasing.

Singers must also learn to vary the quality of their sound. A great
variety of tonal colorings are possible with the human voice. These should
be exploited in the service of the expressive character of the composition.
Beautiful sound is not the final goal in singing—it is simply the means to an
expressive musical end.

CONDUCTING

The most important attribute of the successful conductor is a sense of
authority—the kind of authority based upon confidence in his own abilities
and upon a complete and intimate knowledge of the music. The conductor
must be fully cognizant of all the tonal and dynamic relationships that exist
within the score and he must also be aware of the potential problems that
might develop during the rehearsal of the piece. The conductor must be
sure of his own interpretation. He must have a clear mental image of the
way he wants the piece to sound from the very first tonal impulses to the
last tonal release.

Conducting itself is a practical art. The conductor's job is to realize
the musical images in the clearest, simplest, most vibrant way possible.
During this process, the conductor should feel the music within himself.
He should breathe with the music and try to sense the growth and release of
each tonal impulse. At the same time, he must listen critically to the
results, always comparing the sound he hears to his own mental image of
the piece.

170   *Performance Techniques*

The conductor's movements should emanate from deep within the body. He should avoid the kind of peripheral arm waving and flailing that carries little weight or authority. The conductor should avoid an "all-purpose" beat. His actions should reflect the character of the musical motion as well as the shape of its phrases. Each of his movements should be designed to elicit a particular kind of musical response.

The conductor should practice independence of arm motion. The left hand is especially valuable in indicating the shape of phrases, and shouldn't be confined to cueing or mimicking the movements of the right hand. Cues should indicate the kind of sound as well as the particular performer or section. The conductor should use each gesture to maximum effect. Here again, *focused* energy is the key. Extraneous movements inevitably detract from his effectiveness.

The conductor must gear his actions to the development of the entire composition. He must gauge his motions according to the force and significance of each musical impulse, saving his strongest efforts for the principal climaxes of the work.

The conductor must constantly urge his performers to listen to one another, as if they were playing chamber music. Conductors shouldn't try to impose the sound "from above". They must allow the sound to emerge from within the ensemble, then simply guide and shape the growing musical impulse.

Rehearsal Techniques

The technique of conducting involves the ability to anticipate problems that may develop during the rehearsal of a composition. Some of these problems tend to crop up in most ensembles at one time or another. A few of these are listed below.

Ensemble:

1. Keep a tight ensemble. The larger instruments tend to speak more slowly than the smaller instruments. Don't allow these section to drag. Conversely, don't allow the first violins in an orchestra (or clarinets and flutes in a band) to get ahead of the rest of the ensemble.

2. Maintain a judicious balance between principal lines and subordinate accompaniment parts, as well as between different sections of the group.

3. Maintain uniformity of articulation in tutti passages. Brass performers, for instance, tend to separate notes quite markedly in non-legato passages. String players, on the other hand, tend to produce a more continuous pattern. These two kinds of articulation must be equalized for good ensemble precision.

4. Avoid triplet rhythms in dotted contexts: ♫♫ . To maintain maximum intensity, keep the shorter notes as loud as the dotted notes. (However, if a more relaxed, "jazzy" style is desired, lighten up and loosen up on the 16th notes.) To avoid accenting them, strings normally use a linked or "hook" bowing: ♫♫ .

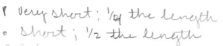

Very short; 1/4 the length

Short; 1/2 the length

Portamento; 3/4 the length

5. Parts that join a line in progress tend to be late. The remedy: "Breathe early and come in on time."

6. After rests downbeat entrances, especially strongly accented entrances, tend to be early. "Wait for the downbeat":

7. Staccato means "short," but not "as short as possible." Vary the length of the staccato according to the style of the music. (In Beethoven's time, vertical slashes or wedges were used to indicate very short, sharply accented notes. These notes were to be held for 1/4th their notated value. Dots indicated that the notes were to receive 1/2 their value. A portato marking (⌢) indicated that the notes were to receive 3/4ths of their value. These distinctions are often blurred in later editions, but the concept of the "long staccato" is an important one in the performance of music from that period.)

8. Declamatory styles, marches, spritely dances, and most Baroque allegro melodies call for a detached style that is neither staccato nor legato. C.P.E. Bach wrote: "The notes that are neither staccato nor legato nor sustained are to be held for half their value, unless the abbreviation 'ten.' stands over them, in which case they must be held."

9. Fermatas don't *necessarily* mean "twice as long as written." Gauge the dynamic implications of the held note and gear your performance accordingly. Don't allow an arbitrary diminuendo on fermatas.

Phrasing:

10. Remember that *all* tones (and most rests) are dynamically significant. Every tone should be set in a larger context. Long notes, too, must be shaped.

11. Always extend the sound into and through the focal point of the phrase.

12. Don't *always* emphasize the highest note of a phrase.

13. Take special care to shape the ends of phrases.

14. Particularly in the notation of early music, little effort is made to distinguish between phrase- and slur-lines. As a result, these distinctions must be made according to the best judgement of the performer.

Dynamics:

15. Maintain a variety of dynamic levels through the piece.

16. Maintain good proportion in long crescendo and decrescendo passages. Spread the change over the entire length of the markings.

17. With few exceptions (notably in the lowest register of oboe and bassoon) soft pianissimos *are* possible within the normal ranges of most instruments. Insist upon this dynamic level when required by the music.

18. Maintain intensity in soft passages, especially in "misterioso" sections.

19. Insist upon clean subito piano attacks. (Sometimes these attacks must be delayed slightly to insure clarity.)

Tone quality:

20. All instruments have an upper dynamic limit at which they can maintain good tone. Do not exceed this limit.

21.   Encourage players to vary their tone quality according to the expressive character of the music.

Conductors must become intimately familiar with the instruments of their ensembles. Orchestral conductors must be particularly familiar with the characteristics of the stringed instruments. Some basic string techniques are listed below.

1.   Whenever possible, bowings should be planned to coincide with the natural characteristics of the bow stroke. As a general rule: ∨ (upbow) = a natural crescendo and is used on most upbeats. ⊓ (downbow) = a natural emphasis and diminuendo and is used on most downbeats. Whenever possible, these basic patterns should be used to reinforce the inherent dynamic implications of the music.

2.   Successive downbows produce a series of detached, accented notes. ⊓ ⊓ ⊓ ⊓ This pattern is also used with successive chords.

3.   Successive upbows produce a series of lighter tones.

4.   The normal pattern of ∨ ⊓ may be reversed to avoid an undue accent on any particular downbeat.

EX. 122   Mozart, *Symphony No. 40,* 1st mvt.

5.   The normal patterns can be reversed to balance out a long crescendo pattern.

EX. 123

6.   Bowing patterns can be altered in repeated phrases to produce a variety of tonal shapings. However, in each case, the dynamic implications of the music should be the principal guiding factor.

Bowing articulation directly affects the character of the musical line. The principal types of articulation are listed below.

1. Legato: Several notes with a single bow. Aim for smooth transition between notes. Avoid unmusical pauses or accents on change of bow.

2. Portato (louré): Each note receives an expressive emphasis through increased bow pressure. (However, the bow does not stop between notes.)

3. Détaché (*not* detached): Separate bow strokes for each note, but the notes themselves are not separated.

4. Martelé (hammered): Marcato. Separate, accented notes. Bow remains on the string, with a little bite or dig into the string on each note.

5. Spiccato: Bow bounces off the string. Just as there are variations in the length of staccato notes, so too spiccato bowing can be varied from a very crisp off-the-string bowing to a more weighty half-on, half-off bowing, depending on the style of the music.

6. Saltando (thrown staccato): A special effect used for quick duplets or triplets. Bow rebounds of its own accord.

EX. 124 Rossini, *William Tell,* Overture

7. Pizzicato (plucked strings): The fleshy part of the finger tip should be used. Care must be taken in loud passages that the string does not rebound against the finger board. The plucking motion should pull the string sideways. In soft, slow passages, resonance can be enhanced through the use of vibrato.

Some specific suggestions for the strings:

1. Attacks that begin with the bow on the string produce a cleaner ensemble.
2. Avoid open strings (especially upper strings) in legato melodies and other exposed situations, unless called for as a special effect.
3. Bowing over the barline often produces a smoother transition.
4. As a general rule, use a full bow in piano as well as forte passages, and vary the bow pressure and the distance from the bridge to produce the appropriate dynamic level. (Shorter strokes are generally better in Baroque styles.)
5. In phrases with a short anacrusis, begin near the middle of the bow.
6. Do not accent the first note of a phrase unless it is called for by the music.
7. Do not crescendo on the last note of a phrase unless it is *musically* desirable.
8. Take care to vibrate at the beginning and end of tones, especially in piano passages.
9. Do not phrase according to the bow; bow according to the phrase.

Choral Conducting

Choral conductors must have a clear understanding of the voice and of the special principles that apply to the choral singer. One of the most important of these is the fact that the vocal quality of the choral singer must be different from that of the soloist. For the choral singer blend is of utmost importance, and wide vibratos and sliding portamentos are particularly inappropriate. The conductor must take special care to match the choral tone to the style of the composition.

Diaphragmatic support and control of the breath is essential in choral singing, as it is in solo performance. It is particularly important in melismatic lines, and in marcato passages. Choral singers should practice use of the "h" in these settings until the proper diaphragmatic techniques are mastered.[5]

Singers should be encouraged to "stagger" their breathing during long musical phrases; however, they should never breathe just before focal points or final resolutions. Intensity of tone must be maintained, especially in soft passages, and in passages that require a maximum of rhythmic precision.

Enunciation is very important in choral singing. The singer must understand that ensemble singing, especially in large ensembles and in choruses accompanied by an orchestra, requires an exaggeration of the normal vocal enunciation if it is to cut through the aggregate sound. The same rules apply here as they do in solo performance. They are as follows:

1. Only pure vowel sounds should be used.
2. When singing diphthongs and final "r's" the last sound should come at the very end of the word.
3. Use a silent "h" before words that begin with a vowel to avoid glottal attacks and improper elisions or slurrings.
4. Emphasize the closed consonants *l, m, ng,* and *n* through increased intensity.
5. Do not voice these consonants when they appear at the end of words.
6. Deemphasize the dental and labial consonants *f, th, s,* and *z.*
7. Enunciate clearly (but do not exaggerate) the plosive consonants *d, t, b,* etc., especially when they appear at the end of words.

Choral conductors must make a special effort to phrase the music. As we have seen in an earlier chapter, this shaping process usually follows the normal accentuation of the text. In this context, special care must be taken to emphasize the accented syllables of the phrase, and *deemphasize* the weaker syllables, especially when these syllables coincide with a natural musical accent.

Exceptions to this rule occur, usually at the end of phrases, when the significance of a particular musical resolution takes precedence. The

[5] See examples 119 and 120.

phrase must then be shaped according to the dynamic implications of the music.[6]

Choral singers, and ensemble performers in general, often think they are phrasing effectively when in fact their efforts may be evident only to themselves and to those nearest to them. These performers must understand that the more subtle aspects of articulation and phrasing that are clearly evident in solo performance are easily lost in ensemble settings. Ensemble performers must learn to exaggerate their expressive shadings somewhat to create the proper balance. In fact, a good rehearsal technique, especially with amateur groups, is to exaggerate *all* shading patterns at first, and once they are mastered, bring them into proper proportion.[7]

THE FINAL EFFECT

As a general rule, the performer must try to become aware of his performance, not as he conceives it to be, but as it is actually heard by the listener, and he must therefore make a continual effort to adjust his performance to the contingencies of each situation. Different halls, for example, possess different acoustical characteristics. Subtle nuances that are effective in a small room or studio may not carry as well in a large auditorium. The performer must be sensitive to the acoustical setting and make the necessary adjustments.

Performers must always strive to maintain a maximum amount of concentration and intensity throughout their performances. Today, performers generally possess a technical level of accomplishment that far exceeds that of a few generations ago. Unfortunately, their performances do not always possess the excitement and drama that typified the great performances of the past. All the surface features are there, but the heart and soul of the music often seem to be lacking.

As we have stated earlier, the performer must continually try to match his actual performance with his mental image of the music, both in terms of the technical aspects of the piece, and in terms of the emotional and spiritual content of the composition. His full attention must constantly be focused on the performance. Accompaniment figures and background patterns must all be shaped with care, for attentive listeners can immediately sense when a sound lacks depth. Every tone must have mental as well as physical presence. Each note must radiate with a warmth and vibrancy that communicates in a very basic way the joy and pleasure of music while, at the same time, revealing the artist's own sincerity and commitment to his art.

---

[6] See Chapter 2, ''Vocal Patterns of Expression,'' for a more detailed discussion of this concept.

[7] Yehudi Menuhin uses this method when practicing for his own solo performances.

Index of Musical
Examples

Bach, J.S.

B Minor Mass, ''Agnus Dei'': p. 48
Brandenburg Concerto No. 2, 3rd mvt.: p. 68
Brandenburg Concerto No. 4, 2nd mvt.: p. 5
Fugue in D Major: pp. 95–96
Little Prelude No. 6: p. 48
Suite in F Major, Bourrée: p. 20
Two-Part Inventions
      Invention No. 1 in C Major: pp. 26–28, 120
      Invention No. 4 in D Minor: pp. 86–87
      Invention No. 14 in B♭ Major: pp. 49–50

Bartok, B.

Concerto for Orchestra, 5th mvt.: pp. 14–15
Mikrokosmos
      Syncopation, No. 133, Vol. V: pp. 65–66
      Dance in Bulgarian Rhythm, No. 151, Vol. VI: p. 66

Beethoven, L. van

Choral Fantasy: p. 118
Piano Concerto No. 1, 1st mvt.: pp. 85–86
Piano Concerto No. 1, 3rd mvt.: pp. 96, 112
Piano Sonata in F Minor, Op. 2 No. 1, 1st mvt.: p. 90
Piano Sonata in A Major, Op. 2 No. 2, 3rd mvt.: pp. 90–91
Piano Sonata in Eb Major, Op. 7, 2nd mvt.: p. 40
Piano Sonata in C Minor (Pathètique), Op. 13, 1st mvt.: p. 106
Piano Sonata in C Minor (Pathètique), Op. 13, 3rd mvt.: p. 21
Piano Sonata in G Minor, Op. 49 No. 1, 1st mvt.: pp. 43, 83
String Quartet in F Major, Op. 18 No. 1, 1st mvt.: pp. 124–32
String Quartet in C Minor, Op. 18 No. 4, 1st mvt.: p. 40
Symphony No. 3, 1st mvt.: pp. 70, 117
Symphony No. 3, 2nd mvt.: pp. 113–14
Symphony No. 3, 3rd mvt.: p. 104
Symphony No. 4, 1st mvt.: p. 34
Symphony No. 5, 1st mvt.: pp. 138–141
Symphony No. 5, 2nd mvt.: pp. 60–61
Symphony No. 5, 3rd mvt.: pp. 62–63, 146–51
Symphony No. 8, 1st mvt.: pp. 24–25, 43, 132–36
Symphony No. 9, 2nd mvt.: pp. 83–85

Berg, A.

Lyric Suite, 3rd mvt.: p. 13

Brahms, J.

Intermezzo, Op. 10 No. 3: p. 97
Symphony No. 3, 3rd mvt.: pp. 59–60
Symphony No. 3, 4th mvt.: pp. 152–57
Symphony No. 4, 1st mvt.: p. 105

Chopin, F.

Polonaise No. 3, Op. 40 No. 1: p. 104
Preludes, Op. 28
    No. 1 in C Major: pp. 57–59, 82

No. 4 in E Minor: pp. 100, 101
No. 6 in B Minor: p. 56–57
No. 7 in A Major: pp. 53–54

Copland, A.

Fanfare for the Common Man: pp. 110–11

Davidovsky, M.

Synchronisms No. 1 for Flute and Electronic Sounds: p. 3

Debussy, C.

Prélude à l'Après-midi d'un Faune: p. 39

Dvořák, A.

New World Symphony, 4th mvt.: pp. 7, 143

Einem, G. Von

Four Piano Pieces, No. 4: pp. 63–65

Franck, C.

Symphony in D Minor, 1st mvt.: pp. 110, 141–42

Handel, G.F.

Messiah
"Every Valley Shall be Exalted": p. 167
"For Unto Us a Child Is Born": p. 167
"Hallelujah Chorus": p. 35
Overture: pp. 108–9

Haydn, F.J.

The Creation: pp. 168–69
Symphony No. 94 ("Surprise"), 2nd mvt.: p. 69

Symphony No. 104, 2nd mvt.: p. 2
Symphony No. 104, 3rd mvt.: pp. 32–33, 70
Symphony No. 104, 4th mvt.: p. 21

Mahler, G.

Symphony No. 1, 2nd mvt.: p. 103
Symphony No. 5, Adagietto: pp. 31–32, 39

Mendelssohn, F.

Midsummer Night's Dream, Overture: p. 8
Ruy Blas, Overture: p. 115
Violin Concerto in E Minor, 1st mvt.: p. 106

Mozart, W.A.

Eine Kleine Nachtmusik, 1st mvt.: p. 44
The Magic Flute, Overture: p. 107
Piano Concerto in C Major, K.503, 1st mvt.: p. 42
Piano Sonata in C Major, K.545, 3rd mvt.: p. 98
Piano Sonata in D Major, K.576, 1st mvt.: p. 92
String Quartet in G Major, K.387, 1st mvt.: p. 67
Symphony No. 40 in G Minor, 1st mvt.: pp. 42, 172
Symphony No. 40 in G Minor, 3rd mvt.: pp. 93–94

Mussorgsky, M.

In the Village: pp. 71–72
"Samuel Goldenberg and Schmuyle," from *Pictures at an Exhibition:* pp. 10–11

Pergolesi, G.B.

Magnificat: pp. 37–38

Ravel, M.

Valses Nobles et Sentimentales, No. I: p. 113
Valses Nobles et Sentimentales, No. VII: pp. 91, 116

Rimsky-Korsakov, N.

Scheherazade: pp. 6, 7

Schoenberg, A.

Sechs Kleine Klavierstücke, Op. 19 No. 4: pp. 33–34

Schubert, F.

Mass in G Major, "Kyrie": p. 36
Symphony No. 5, 1st mvt.: pp. 54–55, 76–78

Schumann, R.

Dichterliebe, No. 1: pp. 52–53, 101, 102–3
Kinderscenen, Op. 15 No. 7, "Traumerei": pp. 55, 75
Piano Concerto in A Minor, 3rd mvt.: p. 97
String Quartet in A Major, 2nd mvt.: p. 41

Strauss, J.

Die Fledermaus: p. 112

Stravinsky, I.

Symphony of Psalms, 2nd mvt.: pp. 25–26

Tchaikowsky, P.I.

Nutcracker, "Valse des Fleurs": p. 119
Romeo and Juliet Overture-Fantasy: p. 5
Symphony No. 4, 2nd mvt.: pp. 22–23, 87–89, 145–46
Symphony No. 5, 1st mvt.: pp. 118, 136–38
Symphony No. 5, 3rd mvt.: p. 117
Symphony No. 6 (Pathètique), 1st mvt.: pp. 3, 12, 51, 144

Wagner, R.

Die Meistersinger, Overture: p. 5
Tristan und Isolde, Prelude: pp. 29–30

Wolf, H.

"Das Verlassene Mägdlein," from *Gedichte von Mörike:* pp. 79–81